J. J. Keller

& Associates, Inc.

Since 1953

3003 W. Breezewood Lane
P.O. Box 368
Neenah, WI 54957-0368
USA

1-800-327-6868

www.jjkeller.com

16-ORS (744)

Driver's Guide
to the
FMCSRs

2nd Edition

J. J. Keller
& Associates, Inc.
Since 1953

INTRODUCTION

Often, the words and phrases used in the Federal Motor Carrier Safety Regulations (FMCSRs) are hard to understand, making it difficult for drivers and their employers to comply with the regulations. The *Driver's Guide to the FMCSRs* is a plain English explanation of the motor carrier safety regulations drivers and their employers must follow.

This book is meant to be used as a companion to the *Federal Motor Carrier Safety Regulations Pocketbook*. It summarizes many of the main points of the FMCSRs, covering the topics that affect drivers.

©2008

J. J. Keller & Associates, Inc.
3003 W. Breezewood Lane, P.O. Box 368
Neenah, Wisconsin 54957-0368
Phone: (800) 327-6868
www.jjkeller.com

Library of Congress Catalog Card Number: 9889359

ISBN 1-57943-367-7

Canadian Goods and Services Tax (GST)
Number: R123-317687

Printed in the U.S.A.

Second Edition, May 2008

Due to the constantly changing nature of government regulations, it is impossible to guarantee absolute accuracy of the material contained herein. The Publishers and Editors, therefore, cannot assume any responsibility for omissions, errors, misprinting, or ambiguity contained within this publication and shall not be held liable in any degree for any loss or injury caused by such omission, error, misprinting or ambiguity presented in this publication.

This publication is designed to provide reasonably accurate and authoritative information in regard to the subject matter covered. It is sold with the understanding that the Publisher is not engaged in rendering legal, accounting, or other professional service. If legal advice or other expert assistance is required, the services of a competent professional person should be sought.

The Editorial Staff is available to provide information generally associated with this publication to a normal and reasonable extent, and at the option of and as a courtesy of the Publisher.

CONTENTS

Federal Motor Carrier Safety Regulations

PART 382 — Controlled Substances and Alcohol Use and Testing 5

PART 40 — Procedures for Transportation Workplace Drug and Alcohol Testing Programs . 42

PART 383 — Commercial Driver's License Standards; Requirements and Penalties 187

PART 391 — Qualifications of Drivers . 225

PART 392 — Driving of Motor Vehicles 259

PART 395 — Hours of Service of Drivers 275

PART 396 — Inspection, Repair, and Maintenance 304

PART 397 — Transportation of Hazardous Materials; Driving and Parking Rules 315

SUBJECT INDEX 322

Reserved

PART 382 — CONTROLLED SUBSTANCES AND ALCOHOL USE AND TESTING

The **exact wording** of the regulations in this section appears in Part 382 of the Federal Motor Carrier Safety Regulations.

Subpart A — General

§382.101 Purpose.

The purpose of Part 382 is to prevent commercial motor vehicle accidents and injuries that are the result of driver misuse of alcohol and/or abuse of drugs.

§382.103 Applicability.

You must follow the drug and alcohol regulations if your vehicle:

√   has a gross combination weight rating (GCWR) of 26,001 or more pounds, inclusive of a towed unit with a gross vehicle weight rating (GVWR) of more than 10,000 pounds;

√   has a GVWR of 26,001 or more pounds;

√ is designed to transport 16 or more passengers, including the driver; or

√ is of any size transporting hazardous materials requiring placarding.

You must also follow the drug and alcohol regulations if you are operating a commercial motor vehicle in the U.S. and are subject to:

√ the Licencia Federal de Conductor (Mexico) requirements; or

√ the commercial driver's license requirements of the Canadian National Safety Code.

If you employ yourself as a driver, you must follow both the requirements that apply to drivers and employers.

Exceptions — The Part 382 requirements do not apply to:

√ employers and drivers required to follow the drug and/or alcohol testing requirements of the Federal Transit Administration (Part 655);

√ military personnel who a state must waive from the commercial driver's license (CDL) requirements of Part 383;

√ operators of farm vehicles who a state has exempted from the Part 383 CDL requirements; and

√ firefighters or other emergency personnel.

§382.105 Testing procedures.

Your employer must be sure that all alcohol and drug tests conducted under Part 382 follow the procedures listed in Part 40.

§382.111 Other requirements imposed by employers.

The Part 382 regulations do not end your employer's authority to include requirements not listed in Part 382.

§382.113 Requirement for notice.

Before an alcohol or drug test may be performed, your employer must notify you that the test is required under the Part 382 regulations. If your employer gives a drug and/or alcohol test that is not required under the Part 382 regulations he/she may not state that it is a test required under the Part 382 regulations.

§382.117 Public interest exclusion.

Your employer may not use the services of a service agent who is subject to a public interest exclusion (PIE). (*see Part 40, Subpart R*)

§382.119 Stand-down waiver provision.

Editor's Note: In Part 382, stand down means you are temporarily removed from the performance of safety-sensitive functions based only on a report from a lab to the medical review officer (MRO) of a confirmed positive, adulterated, or substituted drug test. Your removal from safety-sensitive functions happens before the MRO has completed verification of the test result.

Your employer must receive a waiver from the Federal Motor Carrier Safety Administration (FMCSA) in order to subject you to a stand down. (*see §40.21 for stand down details*)

§382.121 Employee admission of alcohol and controlled substances use.

If your employer chooses to establish a program that allows you to self-identify drug use or alcohol abuse without being subject to the referral, evaluation, and treatment requirements in Part 382 and Part 40 certain criteria must be followed.

Your admission must follow the steps of your employer's voluntary self-identification policy. This policy must be in writing and include the following elements:

1. The policy must prohibit your employer from taking adverse action against you for making a voluntary admission of alcohol misuse or drug use.

2. The policy must allow you sufficient opportunity to seek evaluation, education, or treatment to establish control over your alcohol or drug problem.

3. The policy must permit you to return to safety-sensitive functions only upon the successful completion of an educational or treatment program, as determined by an alcohol and drug abuse evaluation expert (employee assistance professional, substance abuse professional, qualified alcohol and drug counselor, etc.)

4. The policy must ensure that before you return to safety-sensitive functions you undergo a return-to-duty alcohol test with results of less than 0.02 and/or a return-to-duty drug test with a verified negative result.

5. The policy may incorporate monitoring and include non-DOT follow-up testing.

You may not self-identify in order to avoid a test required under Part 382 regulations.

You must make the admission of alcohol misuse or drug use before performing a safety-sensitive function.

You may not perform a safety-sensitive function until your employer is satisfied that you have been evaluated and have successfully completed education or treatment requirements in accordance with the self-identification programs guidelines.

Subpart B — Prohibitions

Editor's Note: In Part 382, a safety-sensitive function means all time from the time you begin work or are required to be ready to work until the time you are relieved from work and all responsibilities for performing work. Safety-sensitive functions include:

√ all time at an employer or shipper plant, terminal, facility, or other property, or on any public property, waiting to be dispatched, unless you have been relieved from duty by your employer;

√ all time inspecting equipment as required by §§392.7 and 392.8 or otherwise inspecting, servicing, or conditioning any commercial motor vehicle at any time;

√ all time spent at the driving controls of a commercial motor vehicle in operation;

√ all time, other than driving time, in or upon any commercial motor vehicle except time resting in a sleeper berth;

√ all time loading or unloading a commercial motor vehicle, supervising or assisting in the loading or unloading, attending a commercial motor vehicle being loaded or unloaded, remaining ready to operate the commercial motor vehicle, or in giving or receiving receipts for shipments loaded or unloaded; and

√ all time repairing, obtaining assistance, or remaining in attendance upon a disabled commercial motor vehicle.

§382.201 Alcohol concentration.

You may not report for duty or remain on duty and perform safety-sensitive functions while having an alcohol level of 0.04 or greater.

§382.205 On-duty use.

You may not use alcohol while performing safety-sensitive functions.

§382.207 Pre-duty use.

You may not perform safety-sensitive functions within 4 hours after using alcohol.

§382.209 Use following an accident.

If you are required to take a post-accident alcohol test (*see §382.303*) you may not use alcohol for 8 hours following the accident, or until you have taken a post-accident alcohol test, whichever happens first.

§382.211 Refusal to submit to a required alcohol or controlled substances test.

You may not refuse to submit to the following alcohol or drug tests:

√ post-accident;

√ random;

√ reasonable suspicion; or

√ follow-up.

Your employer must not allow you to perform or continue to perform safety-sensitive functions if you refuse any of the alcohol or drug tests listed above.

§382.213 Controlled substances use.

You may not report for duty or remain on duty and perform safety-sensitive functions if you have used drugs.

Your employer may also require you to inform him/her of any drugs you are using to treat a medical condition.

Exception — There is an exception to the requirements listed above if you are using a drug under the direction of a licensed medical practitioner, and he/she has advised you that the drug will not affect your ability to safely operate a commercial motor vehicle.

§382.215 Controlled substances testing.

You may not report for duty, remain on duty, or perform a safety-sensitive function if you have a positive, adulterated, or substituted drug test result.

Subpart C — Tests Required

There are six types of tests required under the regulations. All six are listed in Subpart C.

§382.301 Pre-employment testing.

You must undergo a pre-employment drug test before you perform any safety-sensitive function for your employer. You may not perform a safety-sensitive function until you have received a verified negative test result.

Exception — Your employer is not required to carry out a pre-employment drug test if the following conditions are met:

√ you participated in a drug testing program meeting the requirements of Part 382 within the past 30 days;

√ while participating in this program you must have either been tested for drugs in the past 6 months, or have been in the random drug testing pool for the past 12 months; and

√ your employer must make sure that no prior employer has a record of you violating any Department of Transportation (DOT) controlled substance use rule in the past 6 months.

To take advantage of the exception listed above, your new employer must contact the testing program you participated in before using you as a driver and obtain the following information:

√ the name and address of the program (this is generally your prior and/or current employer);

√ verification that you are participating or participated in the program;

√ verification that the program follows the required procedures set forth in Part 40 of the regulations;

√ verification that you are qualified under this rule, including that you have not refused to submit to a drug test;

√ the date you were last tested for drugs; and

√ the results of any drug or alcohol test given in the past 6 months, and any violations of the alcohol misuse or drug use rules.

If your drive for an employer who uses, but does not employ you more than once a year, the employer must check at least every 6 months to verify that you participate in a drug testing program that meets the requirements of the regulations.

Your employer may, but is not required to, conduct pre-employment alcohol testing.

The following requirements must be met if your employer chooses to conduct pre-employment alcohol testing.

1. The pre-employment test must be done before you perform any safety-sensitive function.

2. Your employer must test all drivers. Your employer may not test some drivers and not others.

3. Your employer must conduct the test after making a contingent offer of employment or transfer, subject to your passing the pre-employment alcohol test.

4. All tests must be conducted using the Part 40 procedures.

5. You may not begin performing safety-sensitive functions until a test result of less than 0.04 has been received.

§382.303 Post-accident testing.

Your employer is required to conduct, and you are required to submit, to a post-accident test for alcohol when you are involved in and accident and:

√ any person in the accident has died;

√ when you receive a citation within 8 hours of the accident for a moving traffic violation *and* any person involved in the accident is injured and is immediately taken away from the scene of the accident for medical treatment; or

√ when you receive a citation within 8 hours of the accident for a moving traffic violation *and* a vehicle has been towed away from the accident scene.

You employer is required to conduct, and you are required to submit, to a post-accident test for drugs when you are involved in an accident and:

√ any person in the accident has died;

√ when you receive a citation within 32 hours of the accident for a moving traffic violation *and* any person involved in the accident is injured and is immediately taken away from the scene of the accident for medical treatment; or

√ when you receive a citation within 32 hours of the accident for a moving traffic violation *and* a vehicle has been towed away from the accident scene.

The following table notes when a post-accident test is required.

Type of Accident	Citation Issued to the CMV Driver	Test Must be Performed
Human fatality	YES	YES
	NO	YES
Bodily injury with immediate medical treatment away from the scene.	YES	YES
	NO	NO
Disabling damage to any motor vehicle requiring tow away.	YES	YES
	NO	NO

If the post-accident alcohol test is not given within 2 hours of the accident, your employer must make a record stating why the test was not given.

If the post-accident alcohol test is not given within 8 hours of the accident, your employer must stop all attempts to give the test and make a record stating why the test was not given.

If the post-accident drug test is not given within 32 hours of the accident, your employer must stop all attempts to give the test and make a record stating why the test was not given.

Nothing in the regulations should delay medical attention for those injured in the accident. You are allowed to leave the scene of the accident to get help in responding to the accident, or get emergency medical care.

Your employer must give you the necessary information and instructions to allow you to be tested, or get emergency medical care.

If you are subject to a post-accident alcohol test, you must remain available for testing. If you do not remain available for testing, your employer may consider you to have refused testing.

You must not use alcohol for 8 hours following the accident, or until you have submitted to an alcohol test, whichever occurs first.

Exception — Instead of giving a post-accident test, your employer may substitute a test administered by on-site police or public safety officials. Your employer is allowed to substitute a blood or breath alcohol test and a urine drug test performed by local officials.

Exception — Post-accident testing requirements *do not* apply to incidents involving getting in or out of a parked vehicle, the loading or unloading of cargo, or the use of a passenger vehicle (by an employer) that does not fall under the definition of a commercial motor vehicle.

§382.305 Random testing.

Editor's Note: Many of the random testing requirements are the same for both alcohol and drug testing. Two areas in which the regulations differ are the random testing rate and the time period when a test may be conducted.

Alcohol Testing — The random alcohol testing rate is 10 percent of the average number of driver positions.

Random alcohol testing may only be performed:

√ when you are performing a safety-sensitive function;

√ just before you perform a safety-sensitive function; or

√ just after you perform a safety-sensitive function.

Drug Testing — The random drug testing rate is 50 percent of the average number of driver positions.

Drug testing may be done at any time you are working for your employer.

Selection of Drivers — The selection of drivers for drug and alcohol testing must be made by a scientifically valid method. Scientifically valid methods recognized by the regulations include:

√ a random number table; or

√ a computer-based random number generator that is matched with drivers' Social Security numbers, payroll identification numbers, or other comparable identifying numbers.

Drawing names out of a hat is *not* considered a scientifically valid method.

Each driver selected for random alcohol and drug testing must have an equal chance of being tested each time selections are made.

Also, each driver selected for testing must be tested during the selection period.

To calculate the total number of covered drivers eligible for random testing throughout the year, your company must add the total number of covered drivers eligible for testing during each random testing period and divide that total by the number of random testing periods. (Employers who conduct testing more than once per month only need to compute this total on a once per month basis.)

Only covered employees may be in your company's random testing pool, and all covered employees must be in the random pool.

Editor's Note: A consortium/third party administrator (C/TPA) is defined as a service agent that provides or coordinates one or more drug and/or alcohol testing services for employers. This includes groups of employers who join together to administer, as a single entity, the alcohol and drug testing programs of its members, including a combined random testing pool.

Editor's Note: An employer who employs himself/herself as a driver must implement a random alcohol and drug testing program of two or more drivers in the random selection pool. This requirement can be met by conducting random alcohol and drug testing through a C/TPA.

If your company conducts random alcohol and drug testing through a C/TPA, the number of drivers to be tested may be calculated for each individual employer, or may be based on the total number of drivers covered by the C/TPA.

Your company must ensure that the C/TPA is testing at the appropriate testing rate and that only covered employees are in the random testing pool.

All random testing must be unannounced and testing dates must be spread reasonably throughout the calendar year.

When you are notified that you have been selected for random testing, you must immediately proceed to the test site. If you are performing a safety-sensitive function, other than driving a commercial motor vehicle, at the time of notification, you must stop performing the safety-sensitive function and proceed to the testing site as soon as possible.

§382.307

If, in your current job, you are subject to the random alcohol or drug testing rules of more than one DOT agency, you are subject to the random alcohol and drug testing program of the DOT agency that regulates more than 50 percent of your job.

If your employer is required to conduct random alcohol or drug testing under the rules of more than one DOT agency, your employer may:

√ establish separate pools for random selection, with each pool containing the DOT-covered employees who are subject to testing at the same required minimum annual percentage rate; or

√ randomly select employees for testing at the highest minimum annual percentage rate established for the calendar year by any DOT agency to which the company is subject.

§382.307 Reasonable suspicion testing.

You must submit to an alcohol or drug test when your employer or supervisor has reasonable suspicion to believe you are using drugs or alcohol on the job.

Only one supervisor is required to make the reasonable suspicion determination. The supervisor making the determination must have received the training required in §382.603.

Your supervisor's determination of reasonable suspicion must be based on specific, clearly stated observations of your appearance, behavior, speech, and body odors. Indications of the chronic and withdrawal effects of drugs may also be considered when determining reasonable suspicion for drug testing.

Your company must prepare documentation of your conduct and have it signed by the supervisor who witnessed and made the reasonable suspicion testing determination within 24 hours of the observed behavior, or before the results of the alcohol or drug test are released, whichever is earlier.

Drug Testing — Your employer may require you to take a drug test any time reasonable suspicion exists while you are on duty.

Alcohol Testing — Alcohol testing is authorized *only* if the observations are made during, just before, or just after you perform safety-sensitive functions. The person who makes the determination that reasonable suspicion exists may not conduct the alcohol test.

If a reasonable suspicion alcohol test is not given within 2 hours following the observations, your employer must make a record stating the reasons the alcohol test was not given. If the test was not given within 8 hours, your employer must stop all attempts to give the test, and must make a record stating the reasons the alcohol test was not given.

If reasonable suspicion is observed but a reasonable suspicion test has not yet been given, you can not perform safety-sensitive functions until:

√   an alcohol test is given and your alcohol concentration measures less than 0.02; or

√   24 hours have passed following the determination of reasonable suspicion.

The regulations do not give your employer authority to take any action, other than stated above, against you based solely on your behavior and appearance with no test result. However, your employer may take other action separate from the regulations. (*see §382.111*)

§382.309 Return-to-duty testing.

Return-to-duty testing must follow the procedures outlined in Part 40, Subpart O.

§382.311 Follow-up testing.

Follow-up testing must follow the procedures outlined in Part 40, Subpart O.

Subpart D — Handling of Test Results, Record Retention, and Confidentiality

Your employer is required to keep records of the company's alcohol and drug programs.

§382.401 Retention of records.

Your company's drug and alcohol records must be kept in a secure location with limited (controlled) access. Only authorized personnel may have access to these records.

The amount of time your employer must keep records varies, based on the type of record.

The following records must be kept for **5 years:**

√   alcohol test results indicating a breath alcohol concentration of 0.02 or greater;

√   verified positive drug test results;

√   refusals to submit to required alcohol or drug tests;

√   required calibration of evidential breath testing devices (EBT);

√   driver evaluations and referrals;

√   administration of the alcohol and drug testing program; and

√   annual calendar year summary.

The following records must be kept for **2 years**:

√   records related to the alcohol and drug collection process.

The following records must be kept for **1 year**:

√   negative and cancelled drug test results; and

√   alcohol test results indicating a concentration of less than 0.02.

Records related to the education and training of breath alcohol technicians (BAT), screening test technicians (STT), supervisors, and drivers must be kept by your employer while the individual performs the functions which require the training, plus an additional 2 years after the individual has stopped performing those functions.

Following are the types of records that must be kept.

Records related to the collection process:

√ collection logbooks (if used);

√ documents related to the random selection process;

√ calibration documentation of EBTs;

√ documentation of BAT training;

√ documentation of reasoning for reasonable suspicion testing;

√ documentation of reasoning for post-accident testing;

√ documents verifying a medical explanation for the inability to provide adequate breath or urine for testing; and

√ a copy of each annual calendar year summary.

Records related to the driver's test results:

√ employer's copy of the alcohol test form, including results;

√ employer's copy of the drug test chain of custody and control form;

√ documents sent to the employer by the medical review officer (MRO);

√ documentation of any driver's refusal to submit to a required alcohol or drug test;

√ documents provided by a driver to dispute results of a test; and

√ previous employer drug and alcohol test results.

Documentation of any other violations of Part 382.

Records related to evaluations:

√ records pertaining to a substance abuse professional's (SAP's) determination of a driver's need for assistance; and

√ records concerning a driver's compliance with a SAP's recommendations.

Records related to education and training:

√ materials on drug and alcohol awareness, including a copy of the employer's policy on drug use and alcohol misuse;

√ documentation of compliance with requirement to provide drivers with educational material, including driver's signed receipt of materials;

√ documentation of supervisor training;

√ documentation of training for BATs; and

√ certification that training conducted under this rule complies with all requirements of the rule.

Records related to alcohol and drug testing:

√ agreements with collection site facilities, laboratories, BATs, STTs, MROs, consortia, and third party service providers;

√ names and positions of officials and their role in the employer's alcohol and controlled substance testing program;

√ semi-annual statistical summaries of urinalysis received from certified lab; and

√ the employer's drug test policy and procedures.

Your employer may keep these records at any location, but must be able to make the records available at your company's principal place of business within 2 business days when the records are requested by the Federal Motor Carrier Safety Administration (FMCSA).

§382.405 Access to facilities and records.

Your employer may not release any of your drug or alcohol information except when the release of the information is required by law or authorized by the regulations.

You are allowed to receive any records pertaining to your drug or alcohol tests or related matters if you make a written request. Your employer must provide these records promptly.

Your employer is required to permit access to facilities and records upon the request of a DOT or other regulatory official with proper authority.

Your employer is also allowed to disclose this information to the decision-maker in a lawsuit, grievance, or other proceeding initiated by or on behalf of the individual resulting from an action taken under the regulations.

Your employer may also disclose this information in criminal and civil actions. (*see §40.323*)

Records must also be made available to a new employer or other person after your employer receives a written request from you for specific drug and alcohol information.

§382.407 Medical review officer notifications to the employer.

The MRO must follow the requirements of Part 40, Subpart G when reporting the results of drug tests to your employer.

§382.409 Medical review officer record retention for controlled substances.

The MRO or a third party administrator must keep all dated records and notifications of all verified positive drug test results for at least 5 years. All dated records and notifications of negative and cancelled drug tests must be kept for at least 1 year.

The MRO or a third party administrator may not release your individual drug test results without your specific, written permission. This does not prohibit the MRO or a third party administrator from releasing this information to your employer or regulatory officials with proper authority. (*see Part 40, Subpart G*)

§382.411 Employer notifications.

You must be notified of the results of a pre-employment drug test if you request the results within 60 calendar days of being notified of the disposition of your employment application.

Your employer must notify you of the results of random, reasonable suspicion, and post-accident drug tests if the test results are verified positive. Also, your employer must tell you which drug(s) were verified as positive.

If the MRO is unable to contact you to discuss the results of a drug test, the company's designated employer representative (DER) must make a reasonable effort to contact you and ask you to discuss the results with the MRO. Once the DER has contacted you, he/she must notify the MRO that you have been told to contact the MRO within 72 hours.

§382.413 Inquiries for alcohol and controlled substances information from previous employers.

Your employer must follow the procedures in §40.25 when requesting alcohol and drug information from your previous employers.

Subpart E — Consequences For Drivers Engaging in Substance Use-Related Conduct

§382.501 Removal from safety-sensitive function.

If you have tested positive for drugs, had an alcohol concentration of 0.04 or greater, or refused to be tested, you may not perform and your employer may not allow you to perform any safety-sensitive functions (including driving a commercial motor vehicle).

§382.503 Required evaluation and testing.

As well as being removed from all safety-sensitive functions for testing positive for drugs, having an alcohol concentration of 0.04 or greater, or refusing to be tested, you may not go back to performing safety-sensitive functions (including driving a commercial motor vehicle) until you have completed the evaluation and rehabilitation requirements of Part 40, Subpart O.

§382.505 Other alcohol-related conduct.

If you are found to have an alcohol concentration of 0.02 or greater but less than 0.04, you may not perform any safety-sensitive functions (including driving a commercial motor vehicle) for at least 24 hours.

Your employer may not take further action against you, under these regulations, based solely on an alcohol test result of less than 0.04. This does not prohibit your employer from taking action separate from the regulatory requirements.

§382.507 Penalties.

If you and/or your employer violate the requirements listed in Part 40 or Part 382, you and/or your employer are subject to the penalty provisions found in 49 U.S.C. section 521(b).

Subpart F — Alcohol Misuse and Controlled Substances Use Information, Training, and Referral

§382.601 Employer obligation to promulgate a policy on the misuse of alcohol and use of controlled substances.

Your employer must provide you with educational materials that explain the Part 382 requirements. The materials must also explain your employer's drug and alcohol policies and procedures.

Your employer is required to distribute these materials *prior* to the start of alcohol and drug testing.

You must also receive these materials if you are a new hire or transfer into a driving position. You must sign a receipt stating you received a copy of the materials.

Written notice of availability of the materials must also be provided to union representatives.

§382.601

Information on the following areas must be included in the materials:

√ the name of the person designated by your employer to answer your questions about the materials;

√ the categories of drivers who are subject to Part 382;

√ information about safety-sensitive functions, making clear what period of the work day you are required to follow the Part 382 requirements;

√ specific information on conduct that is prohibited;

√ the circumstances under which you will be tested for alcohol and/or drugs under Part 382;

√ the procedures that will be used to test for alcohol and drugs, protect you and the integrity of the testing process, safeguard the validity of the test results, and ensure that those results are attributed to the correct driver;

√ the requirement that you submit to alcohol and drug tests administered in accordance with Part 382;

√ an explanation of what refusal to submit to an alcohol or controlled substance test means and what will happen if you refuse;

√ the consequences if you are found to have violated Part 382, Subpart B, including the requirement that you be removed immediately from safety-sensitive functions, and procedures under Part 40, Subpart O.

√ the consequences if you are found to have an alcohol concentration of 0.02 or greater but less than 0.04; and

√ information concerning the effects of alcohol and drug use on your health, work, and personal life, signs and symptoms of an alcohol or drug problem (a driver's or a co-worker's), and available methods of intervening when an alcohol or drug problem is suspected, including confrontation, referral to any employee assistance program, and/or referral to management.

§382.603

The materials may also include information on additional employer policies on alcohol and drugs. These additional policies must be clearly identified as based on your employer's independent authority.

Your employer is required to keep the original of the receipt you sign stating you have received the materials. A copy of the receipt may be given to you.

§382.603 Training for supervisors.

Your employer must make sure that all employees who supervise drivers receive the following:

√ 60 minutes of training on alcohol misuse; and

√ 60 minutes of training on drug use.

Supervisors will use the training to determine whether reasonable suspicion exists to require you to undergo reasonable suspicion testing. (*see §382.307*)

The supervisor training must cover physical, behavioral, speech, and performance indicators of probable alcohol misuse and use of drugs.

Recurrent training for supervisors is not required.

§382.605 Referral, evaluation, and treatment.

The referral, evaluation, and treatment procedures in Part 40, Subpart O must be followed.

PART 40 — PROCEDURES FOR TRANSPORTATION WORKPLACE DRUG AND ALCOHOL TESTING PROGRAMS

The ***exact wording*** of the regulations in this section appears in Part 40 of the Federal Motor Carrier Safety Regulations.

Editor's Note: A safety-sensitive function means all time from the time a driver begins work or is required to be in readiness to work until the time he/she is relieved from work and all responsibilities for performing work. Safety-sensitive functions include:

√ all time at an employer or shipper plant, terminal, facility, or other property, or on any public property, waiting to be dispatched, unless the driver has been relieved from duty by the employer;

√ all time inspecting equipment as required by §392.7 and §392.8 or otherwise inspecting, servicing, or conditioning any commercial motor vehicle at any time;

√ all time spent at the driving controls of a commercial motor vehicle in operation;

√ all time, other than driving time, in or upon any commercial motor vehicle except time resting in a sleeper berth as defined by the term sleeper berth;

√ all time loading or unloading a commercial motor vehicle; supervising or assisting in the loading or unloading; attending a commercial motor vehicle being loaded or unloaded; remaining in readiness to operate the commercial motor vehicle; or in giving or receiving receipts for shipments loaded or unloaded; and

√ all time repairing, obtaining assistance, or remaining in attendance upon a disabled commercial motor vehicle.

Subpart A — Administrative Provisions

§40.1 Who does this regulation cover?

Part 40 tells those who conduct drug and alcohol tests required by the Department of Transportation (DOT) how to conduct these tests and what procedures to use.

This regulation covers the activities of:

√ transportation employers;

√ safety-sensitive transportation employees (including self-employed individuals, contractors, and volunteers covered by DOT regulations); and

√ service agents (including collectors, breath alcohol technicians, screening test technicians, laboratories, medical review officers, substance abuse professionals, and consortium/third party administrators).

Subpart B — Employer Responsibilities

§40.11 What are the general responsibilities of employers under this regulation?

Your employer is responsible for:

√ meeting all of the Part 40 requirements and procedures;

√ all actions of the company's officials, representatives, and agents (including service agents) in carrying out the requirements; and

√ making sure all agreements and arrangements between the company and service agents comply with the regulations.

§40.13 How do DOT drug and alcohol tests relate to non-DOT tests?

Department of Transportation (DOT) tests must be completely separate from non-DOT tests. DOT tests are first priority. They must be conducted and completed before a non-DOT test is started.

Only tests specified by Part 40 or DOT agency regulations may be conducted on DOT urine or breath specimens. Additional tests may not be performed.

No one is allowed to change or disregard the results of a DOT test based on the results of a non-DOT test.

Your employer must use the DOT-required custody and control form (CCF) or alcohol testing form (ATF) for all DOT-required drug and alcohol tests. The DOT-required CCF or ATF may *not* be used for non-DOT drug and alcohol tests.

§40.15 May an employer use a service agent to meet DOT drug and alcohol testing requirements?

Your employer may use a service agent to perform the tasks needed to comply with the drug and alcohol regulations.

Your employer is responsible for ensuring that the service agent meets all of the required qualifications.

If your employer uses a service agent, the company is still responsible for complying with the regulations. If a service agent doesn't provide the services required under DOT regulations, your company is subject to sanctions.

§40.17 Is an employer responsible for obtaining information from its service agents?

Yes, your employer is responsible for obtaining the information required by Part 40 from its service agents.

§40.21 May an employer stand down an employee before the MRO has completed the verification process?

Editor's Note: In Part 40, stand down means an employee is temporarily removed from the performance of safety-sensitive functions based only on a report from a lab to the medical review officer (MRO) of a confirmed positive, adulterated, or substituted drug test. The removal of the employee from safety-sensitive functions happens before the MRO has completed verification of the test result.

Unless your employer has received a waiver from the DOT, the company may not stand down an employee.

If your employer has received a waiver, the company may stand down an employee once the MRO receives a lab report of:

√   a confirmed positive drug test;

√   an adulterated test; or

√   a substituted test.

§40.23 What actions do employers take after receiving verified test results?

If your employer receives notice of any of the following you must be immediately removed from performing safety-sensitive functions:

√   a verified positive drug test result;

√   a verified adulterated or substituted drug test result (this is considered a refusal to test); or

√   an alcohol test result of 0.04 or higher.

Your employer should not wait to receive a written report or, in the case of drug testing, the result of a split specimen test.

You must be temporarily removed from performing safety-sensitive functions if your employer receives an alcohol test result of 0.02 to 0.039. Your employer should not wait to receive a written report.

If your employer receives a verified positive, adulterated, or substituted test result, or if you have otherwise violated a DOT agency drug and alcohol regulation, you may not return to performing safety-sensitive functions until you have completed the return-to-duty process.

If your drug test result indicates that your specimen was invalid, a second collection must take place under direct observation. You will not receive advance notice of this second collection.

Your employer must instruct the collector to note on the CCF the same reason for the collection as the original test.

Your employer must not attach additional consequences to the invalid test finding.

Your employer may not alter a drug or alcohol test result transmitted by an MRO, breath alcohol technician (BAT), or consortium/third-party administrator (C/TPA).

§40.25 Must an employer check on the drug and alcohol testing record of employees it is intending to use to perform safety-sensitive duties?

If you are performing safety-sensitive duties for your employer for the first time, your employer must (after getting your written permission), ask for the following information from all of your DOT-regulated employers for the past 2 years:

√ alcohol tests with a result of 0.04 or higher alcohol concentration;

√ verified positive drug tests;

√ refusals to be tested (including verified adulterated or substituted drug test results); and

√ other violations of DOT agency drug and alcohol testing regulations.

All of your DOT-regulated employers for the past 2 years *must* release this information upon receiving your written permission.

All information released must be in a written form that ensures confidentiality.

The company that provides your information must keep a written record of the information released including:

√ date;

√ the party to whom the information was released; and

√ a summary of the information provided.

Also, if you have violated a DOT drug and alcohol regulation, your employer must obtain documentation of your successful completion of DOT return-to-duty requirements, including follow-up tests. You may be asked to provide the return-to-duty information if it cannot be obtained from your previous employer.

The information obtained from a previous employer may include any drug or alcohol test information from previous employers.

If possible, your employer must obtain and review this information *before* you perform any safety-sensitive functions.

If this is not possible, your employer must obtain and review this information as soon as possible. However, if your employer has not obtained the information and has not made and documented a good faith effort to obtain the information within 30 days, you must be removed from all safety-sensitive functions.

If you refuse to give written permission for your employer to obtain the information, your employer may not allow you to perform any safety-sensitive functions.

The employer requesting the information must keep a written, confidential record of all information it receives or of the good faith efforts made to obtain the information. Your employer must keep this information for 3 years from the date you first perform a safety-sensitive function.

Your employer must also ask you whether you have tested positive or refused to test, on any pre-employment test for any employer to which you applied for, but did not obtain safety-sensitive transportation work covered by DOT agency drug and alcohol testing rules during the past 2 years.

If you admit to testing positive or refusing a test you may not perform any safety-sensitive functions until a successful completion of the return-to-duty process is documented.

§40.26 What form must an employer use to report Management Information System (MIS) data to a DOT agency?

Your employer, when required to report MIS data to a DOT agency, must use the form and instructions in Appendix H to Part 40.

§40.27 May an employer require an employee to sign a consent or release in connection with the DOT drug and alcohol testing program?

No. Your employer may not require you to sign a consent, release, waiver of liability, or indemnification agreement with respect to any part of the drug or alcohol testing process covered by Part 40. This includes, but is not limited to:

√ collections;

√ laboratory testing;

√ MRO services; and

√ substance abuse professional (SAP) services.

Subpart C — Urine Collection Personnel

§40.31 Who may collect urine specimens for DOT drug testing?

A collector must meet specific training requirements. (*see §40.33*)

Your immediate supervisor may not act as collector when you are tested, unless no other collector is available and your supervisor is permitted to act as collector under Department of Transportation (DOT) agency drug and alcohol regulations.

An employee working for a Department of Health and Human Services-certified lab may not act as a collector if he/she could link you with a urine specimen, drug testing result, or lab report.

§40.33 What training requirements must a collector meet?

The collector in a DOT drug testing program must be knowledgeable of:

√ the Part 40 requirements;

√ current DOT urine specimen collection guidelines;

√ applicable DOT agency requirements; and

√ any changes to the above information.

A collector must receive qualification training. The training must include instruction on:

√ all steps necessary to complete a collection correctly;

√ the proper completion and transmission of a custody and control form (CCF);

√ "problem" collections;

√ fatal flaws, correctable flaws, and how to correct problems in collections; and

√ the collector's responsibility for maintaining the integrity of the collection process, ensuring the privacy of employees being tested, ensuring the security of the specimen, and avoiding conduct or statements that could be offensive or inappropriate.

Following completion of qualification training, the collector must demonstrate proficiency by completing five consecutive error-free mock collections in front of a qualified collector who will monitor and evaluate the collector's performance.

All collectors must complete refresher training at least once every 5 years.

If a collector makes a mistake in the collection process that causes a test to be cancelled, he/she must undergo error correction training within 30 days.

All collectors must keep documentation showing they meet all of the training requirements.

Subpart D — Collection Sites, Forms, Equipment and Supplies Used in DOT Urine Collections

§40.41 Where does a urine collection for a DOT drug test take place?

The collection site must meet all security requirements. (*see §40.43*)

It must have all necessary personnel, materials, equipment, facilities, and supervision to provide for the collection, temporary storage, and shipping of urine specimens to a lab. It must also have a suitable, clean surface for writing.

The collection site may be in:

√   a medical facility;

√   a mobile facility;

√   a dedicated collection facility; or

√   any other location meeting the requirements.

The collection site must have one of the following types of facilities for urination.

1. The first, and preferred, type of facility is a single-toilet room, having a full-length privacy door.

    You are the only person allowed in the room during collection, unless the collection must be directly observed. Then, an observer must be in the room.

    A source of water for washing hands must be available. If the source is in the room where collection will take place, all sources of water, and all other items that could be used for adulteration and substitution must be secured. In this case, a hand washing source or moist towelettes must be outside the room.

2. The second type of facility is a multistall restroom. This collection site must provide substantial visual privacy.

   When a multistall restroom is used the collector must either:

√ secure all sources of water and other items that could be used for adulteration or substitution and place blueing agents in all toilets or secure the toilets to prevent access; or

√ conduct all collections in the facility as monitored collections.

Unless the collection is monitored, or must be directly observed, you are the only person allowed in the multistall restroom.

§40.43 What steps must operators of collection sites take to protect the security and integrity of urine collections?

Collectors and operators of collection sites must take steps to prevent unauthorized access that could compromise the integrity of collections.

The collector must do the following before each collection to deter specimen tampering:

√ secure any water sources or otherwise make them unavailable;

√ ensure that the water in the toilet is blue;

√ ensure that no soap, disinfectants, cleaning agents, or other possible adulterants are present;

√ inspect the collection site to ensure that no foreign or unauthorized items are present;

√ tape or otherwise secure shut any movable toilet tank top, or put bluing in the tank;

√ ensure that undetected access is not possible;

√ secure areas and items that appear suitable for concealing contaminants; and

√ recheck all of the steps listed above after each collection to ensure the collection site's continued integrity.

If the collection site uses a facility normally used for other purposes (public restroom, hospital examining room) the collector must ensure before the collection that:

√ access to collection materials and specimens is restricted; and

√ the facility is secured against access during the procedure to ensure privacy and prevent distraction of the collector.

Limited access signs must be posted.

The collector may only conduct one collection at a time. The only time a second collection may be done at the same time is in a "shy bladder" situation, when one of the collections being conducted is in the period for drinking fluids. (*see §40.193*)

The collector should keep your collection container in his/her view and your view from the time you fill the container until the container is sealed.

The collector must ensure that you and the collector are the only people that handle the specimen before it is poured into bottles and sealed with tamper-evident seals.

You and the collector must remain within the collection site from the time you give the specimen to the collector until the specimen is sealed.

The collector must be in control of your specimen and the custody and control form (CCF) throughout the collection process.

The collection site operator must have policies and procedures that prevent unauthorized personnel from entering any part of the collection site in which urine specimens are collected or stored.

Authorized personnel includes:

√ employees being tested;

√ collectors and other collection site workers;

√ designated employer representatives (DERs);

√ employee and employer representatives authorized by the employer; and

√ Department of Transportation (DOT) agency representatives.

Only the observer in a directly observed collection or the monitor in the case of a monitored collection are permitted to enter the urination facility in which you provide a specimen.

All authorized persons must be under the supervision of a collector at all times when permitted into the site.

The collector may remove any person who obstructs, interferes with, or causes a delay in the collection process.

The collection site operator must keep the number of people handling specimens to a minimum.

§40.45 What form is used to document a DOT urine collection?

The CCF must be used to document every urine collection required by the DOT drug testing program.

The CCF is a five-part carbonless manifold form that may not be modified. There are some exceptions for including certain information including billing and DOT agency information.

The CCF may not transmit personal information that would identify you (other than a Social Security number or other employee identification number) to the drug testing lab.

An equivalent foreign language form may be used if both you and the collector can understand and use the form in that language.

A non-federal form or an expired federal form (the old 7-part federal CCF) may not be used to conduct a DOT urine collection.

§40.47 May employers use the CCF for non-federal collections or non-federal forms for DOT collections?

No, your employer is prohibited from using the CCF for non-federal urine collections and from using non-federal forms for DOT urine collections. Doing either of the above subjects your employer to enforcement action under DOT agency regulations.

In a rare case (by mistake or as the only way to conduct a test under difficult circumstances), if a non-federal form for a DOT-collection is used it is considered a "correctable flaw." In this case the lab may not reject the specimen for testing and the medical review officer (MRO) may not cancel the test result.

The MRO must correct the problem by following the procedures outlined in §40.205.

§40.49 What materials are used to collect urine specimens?

A collection kit meeting the requirements in Part 40, Appendix A must be used.

§40.51 What materials are used to send urine specimens to the laboratory?

A shipping container that protects the specimen bottles from shipment damage must be used. A shipping container is not required if a lab courier hand-delivers the specimens from the collection site to the lab.

Subpart E — Urine Specimen Collections

§40.61 What are the preliminary steps in the collection process?

The collector must take the following steps before beginning a collection:

1. If a specific time has been scheduled for your test, and you do not appear at the collection site, the designated employer representative (DER) will be contacted to determine what time period is acceptable for your arrival. If your arrival is delayed beyond that time, the collector must notify the DER.

   In the case where a consortium/third party administrator (C/TPA) has notified an owner-operator or other employee to report for testing and he/she does not appear, the C/TPA must notify the employee that he/she has refused to test.

2. Once you enter the collection site, the testing process must begin without delay.

If you are taking both the alcohol and drug test, if at all possible, the alcohol test must be completed before the drug test begins.

If you need medical attention, treatment should not be delayed in order to complete a drug test.

You may not be catheterized in order to collect the required urine specimen. The only exception is for an individual who normally voids through self-catheterization. If an individual who normally voids through self-catheterization declines to do so he/she will be considered to have refused a drug test.

3. You must provide positive identification. This includes, but is not limited to, a company issued photo ID or a driver's license. Faxes or photocopies are not acceptable. Positive identification by your employer is also acceptable.

4. You may ask the collector for identification as well.

5. The collector must explain the basic collection procedure to you, including showing you the instructions on the back of the custody and control form (CCF).

6. The collector will direct you to remove outer clothing (coat, hat, coveralls, etc.) that could be used to conceal items or substances that could be used to tamper with a specimen.

   You will be directed to leave all outer clothing as well as any other purse, briefcase, or other belongings in a mutually agreeable location. Failure to do so constitutes a refusal to test.

   You may ask for, and the collector must provide a receipt for belongings.

   You may keep your wallet.

   The collector may not ask you to remove other clothing (shirts, pants, etc.), to remove all clothing, or change into a hospital or examination gown (unless the urine collection is in connection with a Department of Transportation (DOT) agency-authorized medical examination).

You must also empty your pockets and display the items in them to the collector to ensure that no items present could be used to adulterate a specimen. If nothing is there that can be used to adulterate a specimen, you can place the items back in your pocket.

If the collector finds materials that could be used to tamper with a specimen he/she must determine if they were brought with the intent to alter the specimen. If the collector determines that this is the case, a collection under direct observation must be conducted.

If the collector determines that the material was inadvertently brought to the collection site, the collector must secure and maintain it until the collection process is complete. A normal (unobserved) collection may be conducted.

7. You are not to list medications you are currently taking on the CCF.

§40.63 What steps does the collector take in the collection process before the employee provides a urine specimen?

The collector must take the following steps before you provide the urine specimen:

1. Complete Step 1 on the CCF.

2. Instruct you to wash and dry your hands. At this point, you will not have access to water or other materials that could be used to adulterate or dilute a specimen. You may not wash your hands again until you have given the specimen to the collector.

3. The collector must select, or allow you to select, an individually wrapped or sealed collection container. Either you or the collector (with both of you present) must unwrap or break the seal of the collection container.

4. You will be directed by the collector to go into a room used for urination and provide a specimen of at least 45mL, not flush the toilet, and return to the collector with the specimen.

Except in the case of a monitored collection, no one is allowed in the room with you.

Also, the collector may set a reasonable time limit for providing the specimen.

5. The collector must pay careful attention to you during the entire collection process to note any conduct that clearly indicates an attempt to tamper with a specimen.

If the collector detects such conduct, the collection must take place immediately under direct observation. The collector must note the conduct and the fact the collection was observed on the CCF.

As soon as possible, the collector must inform the DER and the collection site supervisor that the collection took place under direct observation and the reason for doing so.

§40.65 What does the collector check for when the employee presents a specimen?

The collector must check the following when you give the collection container to him/her:

1. **Sufficiency of specimen.** The specimen
   must contain at least 45mL of urine. If
   the specimen contains less than 45mL of
   urine, the collector must follow "shy bladder" procedures. (*see §40.193*)

   When following "shy bladder" procedures,
   the original specimen must be discarded
   (unless another problem exists).

   Combining urine from separate voids to
   create a specimen is not permitted.

   Excess urine must be discarded.

2. **Temperature.** The collector must check
   the temperature of the specimen no later
   than 4 minutes after you have given
   him/her the specimen.

   The acceptable temperature range is
   90°-100° F/32°-38° C.

   The collector must determine the temperature by reading the temperature strip
   attached to the collection container.

   The collector must record whether the
   specimen temperature is within the acceptable range on the CCF.

If the specimen temperature is outside the acceptable range, a new collection must be conducted immediately using direct observation procedures. (*see §40.67*)

In a case where a specimen is collected under direct observation because of the temperature being out of range, both the original and directly observed specimen must be processed and sent to the lab. The DER must be notified of the direct observation and the reason for it.

If you refuse to provide another specimen or refuse to provide another specimen under direct observation, the collector must notify the DER and any previous specimen you provided must be discarded.

3. **Signs of tampering.** The collector must inspect the specimen you provide for:

√   unusual color;

√   the presence of foreign objects or materials; or

√   other signs of tampering.

If it is apparent from this inspection that you tampered with the specimen, the collector must immediately conduct a new collection using direct observation procedures.

If a specimen is collected under direct observation because of signs of tampering, both the original and directly observed specimen must be processed and sent to the lab. The DER must be notified of the direct observation and the reason for it.

If you refuse to provide another specimen under direct observation, the collector must notify the DER and any previous specimen you provided must be discarded.

§40.67 When and how is a directly observed collection conducted?

Your employer must order an immediate collection under direct observation with no advance notice if:

√ the lab reports to the medical review officer (MRO) that your specimen is invalid and the MRO reports to your employer that there isn't an adequate medical explanation for the result;

√ the MRO reports to your employer that the original positive, adulterated, or substituted test result has to be cancelled because the test of the split specimen cannot be performed; or

√ the lab reports to the MRO that the specimen was negative-dilute with a creatinine concentration greater than or equal to 2 mg/dL but less than or equal to 5 mg/dL and the MRO reports to your employer that the specimen is negative-dilute.

Your employer may order a collection under direct observation if the drug test is a return-to-duty or follow-up test.

Your employer must explain to you the reason for the directly observed collection.

A collector must immediately conduct a collection under direct observation if:

√ the collector is directed to do so by the DER;

√ the collector observes materials brought to the collection site *or* your conduct clearly indicates an attempt to tamper with a specimen;

√ the temperature on the original specimen is out of range; or

√ the original specimen appears to be tampered with.

The collector must explain to you the reason for the directly observed collection.

The collector must complete a new CCF for the directly observed collection.

In a directly observed collection, the observer must be of the same gender. An opposite gender person may not act as an observer. The observer may be a different person from the collector and doesn't need to be a qualified collector.

In a directly observed collection, the observer must watch you urinate into the collection container. The observer may not take the collection container from you, but must observe the specimen as you take it to the collector.

If you refuse to participate in a directly observed collection, this is considered a refusal to test.

When the collector learns that a directly observed collection should have occurred, but did not, the collector must inform your employer that you must have an immediate recollection under direct observation.

§40.69 How is a monitored collection conducted?

The collector must secure the room being used for a monitored collection so that no one except you and the monitor can enter the room until the collection has been completed.

The monitor must be the same gender as you, unless the monitor is a medical professional (nurse, doctor, physician's assistant). The monitor can be a different person from the collector and doesn't need to be a qualified collector.

A monitor does not watch you urinate into the collection container. He/she listens for sounds or makes other observations that indicate an attempt to tamper with a specimen. If there are signs of attempting to tamper with a specimen, a direct observation collection will be ordered.

The monitor must ensure that you take the collection container directly to the collector as soon as you exit the enclosure.

If you refuse to participate in a monitored collection, this is considered a refusal to test.

§40.71 How does the collector prepare the specimens?

All collections must be split specimen collections.

The collector must take the following steps (in order), in front of you, after you bring the urine specimen to the collector.

1. Check the box on the CCF indicating this is a split specimen collection.

2. Pour at least 30mL of urine from the collection container into one specimen bottle to be used as the primary specimen.

3. Pour at least 15mL of urine from the collection container into a second specimen bottle to be used as the split specimen.

4. Place and secure the lids/caps on the bottles.

5. Seal the bottles by placing tamper-evident bottle seals over the bottle caps/lids and down the sides of the bottles.

6. Write the date on the tamper-evident bottle seals.

7. The collector must then ensure that you initial the tamper-evident bottle seals. This certifies that the bottles contain the specimen you provided. If you refuse to do this, the collector must note this on the CCF and complete the collection process.

8. The collector must discard any urine left over in the collection container after both specimen bottles have been appropriately filled and sealed.

No one (including the collector) may conduct further testing (such as adulteration testing) on this excess urine and you cannot ask that the excess urine be turned over to you.

Exception — The collector may use the excess urine to conduct clinical tests (protein, glucose, etc.) if the collection was conducted in conjunction with a physical exam required by a DOT agency regulation.

§40.73 How is the collection process completed?

The collector completes the collection process by directing you to provide your name, date of birth, and telephone number and sign the CCF. The collector will also provide some data on the CCF.

The collector will then place the specimen bottles and a copy of the CCF in a plastic bag and then secure the bag.

At that point, the collector will advise you that you may leave the collection site.

Then the collector must finish preparing the specimens for shipment to the testing lab.

The specimens must be shipped to the lab as quickly as possible. They must be shipped within 24 hours or during the next business day.

Subpart F — Drug Testing Laboratories

§40.81 What laboratories may be used for DOT drug testing?

A lab located in the U.S. is permitted to participate in Department of Transportation (DOT) drug testing if it is certified by the Department of Health and Human Services (HHS) under the National Laboratory Certification program (NLCP).

A lab located in Canada or Mexico is permitted to participate in DOT drug testing if:

√ the DOT has approved the lab as meeting HHS lab certification standards;

√ the DOT has deemed the lab fully equivalent to a lab meeting HHS standards; or

√ the DOT has recognized a Canadian or Mexican certifying organization as having equivalent lab certification standards and procedures as those of HHS, and the lab was approved by one of those organizations.

All laboratories participating in the DOT drug testing program must comply with all Part 40 and HHS requirements.

If DOT determines that a lab does not comply with the requirements, the lab could be subject to public interest exclusion (PIE) proceedings. (*see Subpart R*)

§40.83 How do laboratories process incoming specimens?

The lab must follow all HHS guidelines for processing specimens.

The lab must inspect each specimen and custody and control form (CCF) for "fatal flaws" including:

√ ID numbers on the specimen and CCF that do not match;

√ a broken seal on the specimen bottle or other signs of tampering;

√ information omitted from the CCF; and

√ an insufficient amount of urine in the primary bottle.

If any of the above "fatal flaws" are found, this must be documented and the testing process stopped.

The lab must inspect each CCF, making sure the collector's signature is on the document. If the collector's signature is missing, the lab must document the flaw and continue the testing process.

In this case, the lab must keep the specimen for at least 5 business days. The lab must attempt to correct the flaw by following certain procedures. (*see §40.205*)

If the flaw is not corrected, the lab must report the result as rejected. (*see §40.97*)

If the lab determines that the specimen temperature was not checked, and the CCF did not include an entry regarding the temperature being out of range, the lab must attempt to correct the problem using certain procedures. (*see §40.208*)

In this case, the lab must continue its efforts to correct the problem for 5 business days before reporting the result.

When the lab receives the correction, or 5 business days have passed, the result must be reported following certain procedures. (*see §40.97*)

If the lab determines that a CCF fails to meet regulatory requirements (non-federal form, expired federal form, etc. (*see §40.45*)), the lab must attempt to correct this by following certain procedures. (*see §40.205*)

If this is the case, the lab must keep the specimen for at least 5 business days.

There are also procedures labs must follow if the split specimen is not shipped with the primary specimen, if the specimen leaks during shipment, and if the lab tests the split specimen as the primary specimen.

§40.85 What drugs do laboratories test for?

The lab must test for the following five drugs:

√ marijuana metabolites;

√ cocaine metabolites;

√ amphetamines;

√ opiate metabolites; and

√ phencyclidine (PCP).

The lab may not test "DOT specimens" for any other drugs.

§40.87 What are the cutoff concentrations for initial and confirmation tests?

The lab must use the cutoff concentrations listed below. (All cutoff concentrations are listed in nanograms per milliliter (ng/mL).

Type of drug or metabolite	Initial test	Confirmation test
(1) Marijuana metabolites ...	50	
(i) Delta-9-tetrahydrocanna-binol-9-carboxylic acid (THC)		15
(2) Cocaine metabolites (Benzoylecgonine)	300	150
(3) Phencyclidine (PCP)	25	25
(4) Amphetamines	1000	
(i) Amphetamine		500
(ii) Methamphetamine		500 (Specimen must also contain amphetamine at a concentration of greater than or equal to 200 ng/mL.)
(5) Opiate metabolites	2000	
(i) Codeine		2000

Type of drug or metabolite	Initial test	Confirmation test
(ii) Morphine		2000
(iii) 6-acetylmorphine (6-AM)		10 (Test for 6-AM in the specimen. Conduct this test only when specimen contains morphine at a concentration greater than or equal to 2000 ng/mL.)

On an initial drug test, if the result is below the cutoff concentration, it is reported as negative. If the result is at or above the cutoff concentration, the lab must conduct a confirmation test.

On a confirmation drug test, if the result is below the cutoff concentration, it is reported as negative. If the result is at or above the cutoff concentration, it is reported as confirmed positive.

The lab must also report quantitative values for morphine or codeine at 15,000ng/mL or above.

§40.89 What is validity testing, and are laboratories required to conduct it?

Specimen validity testing is the evaluation of the specimen to determine if it is consistent with normal human urine.

The purpose of validity testing is to determine:

√ whether certain adulterants or foreign substances were added to the urine;

√ if the urine was diluted; or

√ if the specimen was substituted.

Labs are authorized to conduct validity testing.

§40.91 What validity tests must laboratories conduct on primary specimens?

The lab must determine the creatinine concentration on each primary specimen. The specimen's specific gravity must also be determined if the creatinine concentration is less than 20mg/dL.

The lab must determine the pH of each primary specimen.

The lab must perform one or more validity tests for oxidizing adulterants on each primary specimen.

The lab must perform additional validity tests on the primary specimen when the following conditions are observed:

- Abnormal physical characteristics;

- Reactions or responses characteristic of an adulterant obtained during initial or confirmatory drug tests; or

- Possible unidentified interfering substance or adulterant.

If the lab determines that the specimen is invalid and HHS guidelines direct the lab to contact the MRO, the lab and MRO must together decide if testing the primary specimen by another HHS certified laboratory would be useful in being able to report a positive or adulterated test result.

§40.93 What criteria do laboratories use to establish that a specimen is dilute or substituted?

The lab must consider the primary specimen to be dilute if the creatinine concentration is greater than or equal to 2 mg/dL but less than 20mg/dL, and the specific gravity is greater than 1.0010 but less than 1.0030 on a single aliquot.

The lab must consider the primary specimen to be substituted if the creatinine concentration is less than 2mg/dL *and* the specific gravity is less than or equal to 1.0010 or greater than or equal to 1.0200 on both the initial and confirmatory creatinine tests and on both the initial and confirmatory specific gravity tests on two separate aliquots.

§40.95 What criteria do laboratories use to establish that a specimen is adulterated?

The lab must consider the primary specimen to be adulterated if:

√ a substance that is not expected to be present in human urine is identified in the specimen;

√ a substance that is expected to be in human urine is identified at a concentration so high that it is not consistent with human urine; or

√ the physical characteristics of the specimen are outside the normal expected range of human urine.

When making this determination, the lab must apply current HHS criteria.

§40.97 What do laboratories report and how do they report it?

The lab must report the results for each primary specimen tested as one or more of the following:

√ negative;

√ negative-dilute, with numerical values for creatinine and specific gravity;

√ rejected for testing, with remark(s);

√ positive, with drug(s)/metabolite(s) noted;

√ positive, with drug(s)/metabolite(s) noted—dilute;

√ adulterated, with numerical values (when applicable), with remark(s);

√ substituted, with numerical values for creatinine and specific gravity; or

√ invalid result, with remark(s).

The lab must report results directly, and only to the medical review officer (MRO) at his/her place of business. The results may not be reported through the designated employer representative (DER) or a service agent.

The results report may be transmitted by any means that assures accuracy and confidentiality.

The lab and MRO must ensure that all transmitted results are protected from unauthorized access or release. This applies to both transmission and storage of the results.

The lab must transmit the results in a timely manner, preferably the same day that the review by the certifying scientist is completed.

The lab must provide quantitative values for confirmed positive drug test results to the MRO when requested (in writing) to so by the MRO.

The lab must provide the numerical values that support the adulterated (when applicable) or substituted result, without a request from the MRO.

The lab must also provide the MRO numerical values for creatinine and specific gravity for a negative-dilute test result, without a request from the MRO.

§40.99 How long does the laboratory retain specimens after testing?

The lab must keep a primary specimen that was reported with positive, adulterated, substituted, or invalid results for at least 1 year.

The specimen must be kept in secure, long-term storage in accordance with HHS guidelines.

The specimen may be discarded at the end of 1 year if the lab hasn't received any written requests to retain the specimen for a longer time period.

The split specimen must be kept for the same time period as the primary specimen.

A lab that tests a split specimen must follow the same retention requirements as a lab that tests a primary specimen.

§40.101 What relationship may a laboratory have with an MRO?

A lab may not enter into any relationship with an MRO that creates a conflict of interest with the MRO's responsibilities for the employer.

The lab may not receive any financial benefit by having an employer use a specific MRO.

Examples of conflicts of interest include:

√ a lab that employs an MRO who reviews test results produced by the lab;

√ a lab that gives employers a discount or other incentive to use a particular MRO; or

√   a lab that has a contract or retainer with an MRO for the review of test results produced by the lab.

§40.103 What are the requirements for submitting blind specimens to a laboratory?

An employer or consortium/third party administrator (C/TPA) with an aggregate of 2,000 or more DOT-covered employees must send blind specimens to the labs it uses.

An employer or C/TPA with an aggregate of fewer than 2,000 DOT-covered employees is not required to provide blind specimens.

When submitting blind specimens, a certain number of specimens must be sent, with about 75 percent being blank and 15 percent being positive for one or more of the prohibited drugs. (*see §40.103*)

§40.109 What documentation must the laboratory keep, and for how long?

The lab must retain all employee urine specimen records and all employer-specific data (*see §40.111*) for at least 2 years.

The records may be discarded at the end of the 2 year period if the lab hasn't received any written requests to retain the records for a longer time period.

§40.111 When and how must a laboratory disclose statistical summaries and other information it maintains?

The lab must submit an aggregate statistical summary to the employer semiannually.

The summary may not reveal the identity of any employee.

For confidentiality purposes, the lab may not send a summary if the employer has fewer than five test results.

The lab must provide a summary when the employer requests it in response to an inspection, audit, or review by a DOT agency. Again, for confidentiality purposes, the lab may not send a summary if the employer has fewer than five aggregate test results.

Subpart G — Medical Review Officers and the Verification Process

§40.121 Who is qualified to act as an MRO?

To be qualified to act as a medical review officer (MRO), an individual must meet the following requirements:

1. **Credentials.** An MRO must be a licensed physician (Doctor of Medicine or Osteopathy).

2. **Basic knowledge.** An MRO must be knowledgeable about and have clinical experiences in controlled substances abuse disorders, including detailed knowledge of alternative medical explanations for lab confirmed drug test results.

He/she must be knowledgeable about issues relating to adulterated and substituted specimens as well as the possible medical causes of specimens having an invalid result.

He/she must be knowledgeable about the Part 40 regulations, the Department of Transportation (DOT) MRO Guidelines, and the applicable DOT agency regulations.

3. **Qualification training.** The MRO must receive qualification training on:

√ collection procedures for urine specimens;

√ chain of custody, reporting, and record-keeping;

√ interpretation of drug and validity test results;

√   the role and responsibilities of the MRO in the DOT drug testing program;

√   the interaction with other participants in the program; and

√   provisions of Part 40 and DOT agency rules applying to employers for whom the MRO reviews test results including updates and changes.

Following the completion of qualification training the MRO must successfully pass an exam administered by a nationally-recognized MRO certification board.

4. **Continuing education.** Once every 3 years an MRO must complete at least 12 professional hours of continuing education related to performing MRO functions.

5. **Documentation.** The MRO must maintain documentation showing that he/she currently meets all of the requirements. This information must be provided on request to DOT agency representatives and employers and consortium/third party administrators (C/TPAs) who are using or negotiating to use the MRO's services.

§40.123 What are the MRO's responsibilities in the DOT drug testing program?

The MRO must act as an independent and impartial "gatekeeper" and advocate for the accuracy and integrity of the drug testing process.

The MRO must provide a quality assurance review of the drug testing process for the specimens under his/her control. This includes, but is not limited to:

√ ensuring the review of the custody and control form (CCF) on all specimen collections for the purposes of determining whether there is a problem that may cause a test to be cancelled;

√ providing feedback to employers, collection sites, and laboratories regarding performance issues where necessary; and

√ reporting to and consulting with a relevant DOT agency when the MRO wants DOT assistance in resolving a program issue.

The MRO must determine whether there is a legitimate medical explanation for confirmed positive, adulterated, substituted, or invalid drug test results from the lab.

The MRO must act to investigate and correct problems where possible, and notify appropriate parties where assistance is needed.

The MRO must ensure the timely flow of test results and other information to employers and provide confidentiality of the drug testing information.

§40.125 What relationship may an MRO have with a laboratory?

The MRO may not enter into any relationship with an employer's lab that creates a conflict of interest or an appearance of a conflict of interest.

The MRO may not receive financial benefit by having an employer use a specific lab.

§40.127 What are the MRO's functions in reviewing negative test results?

The MRO must review the CCF for fatal or correctable errors.

The MRO must review negative lab test results and ensure they are consistent with the information on the CCF.

Once the MRO has determined that the CCF is accurate and legible he/she must check the "negative" box on the CCF, provide his/her name, sign, initial, or stamp, and date the verification statement.

Then, the MRO must report the result in a confidential manner.

§40.129 What are the MRO's functions in reviewing laboratory confirmed positive, adulterated, substituted, or invalid drug test results?

The MRO must review the CCF for fatal or correctable errors.

The MRO must review the CCF making sure the test result is legible and that the certifying scientist signed the form.

Then, the MRO must conduct a verification interview. This interview must include direct contact, in person, by telephone between the MRO and you. The MRO may start the verification process based on the lab results report.

The MRO must verify the test result as either:

√ negative;

√ positive;

√ cancelled; or

√ refusal because of adulteration or substitution.

In the case of a positive test result, once the MRO has determined that the CCF is accurate and legible he/she must check the "positive" box on the CCF, indicate the drug(s)/metabolite(s) detected, and sign and date the verification statement.

Then, the MRO must report the result in a confidential manner.

In the case of a lab confirmed positive, adulterated, substituted, or invalid drug test that has been cancelled, the MRO must check the "cancelled" box on the CCF, make the appropriate notes in the remarks section, and sign and date the verification statement.

In the case of a substituted or adulterated test result, the MRO must check the "refusal to test because:" box on the CCF, check the "adulterated" or "substituted" box, as appropriate, make the appropriate notes in the remarks section of the CCF, and sign, and date the verification statement.

If your employer has a stand-down policy, the MRO may report to the designated employer representative (DER) that the MRO has received an employee's confirmed positive, adulterated, or substituted result, consistent with the terms of the waiver the employer received. The MRO may not provide any further details about the test result.

If your employer does not have a stand-down policy, the MRO may not inform your employer that the MRO has received a confirmed positive, adulterated, or substituted result.

§40.131 How does the MRO or DER notify an employee of the verification process after a confirmed positive, adulterated, substituted, or invalid test result?

When the MRO receives a confirmed positive, adulterated, substituted, or invalid test result from the lab, he/she must contact you directly, on a confidential basis, to determine whether you want to discuss the test result.

During this conversation, the MRO must explain to you that if you decline to discuss the result, the MRO will verify the test as positive or a refusal to test.

Staff under the personal supervision of the MRO may conduct this initial contact in order to schedule an appointment for you and the MRO. This staff person may not gather medical information or discuss the test result.

A reasonable effort must be made to contact you. Reasonable efforts include a minimum of three attempts spaced reasonably over a 24-hour period to the telephone number(s) you provided on the CCF.

If you cannot be reached, the MRO must take the following steps:

√ document the attempts to reach you including dates and times; and

√ contact the DER, asking him/her to let you know you need to get in contact with the MRO. (No additional information (test results, etc.) may be shared with the DER.)

The DER must attempt to contact you immediately, using procedures that protect, as much as possible, the confidentiality of the MRO's request.

If the DER does contact you, the DER must document the date and time of the contact and notify the MRO.

The DER will tell you that you must contact the MRO immediately. The DER will tell you the consequences of failing to do so within the next 72 hours.

If the DER makes reasonable efforts to contact you, but fails to do so, your company may place you on temporary medically unqualified status or medical leave.

A reasonable effort is a minimum of three attempts, spaced reasonably, over a 24-hour period to the telephone number(s) you provided on the CCF. The DER must document the dates and times of these efforts.

If the DER cannot contact you within 24 hours, he/she must leave a message (mail, e-mail, voice mail) for you to contact the MRO. The DER must also inform the MRO of the date and time of the attempted contact.

§40.133 Under what circumstances may the MRO verify a test as positive, or as a refusal to test because of adulteration or substitution, without interviewing the employee?

Normally, the MRO may verify a confirmed positive test or a refusal to test because of adulteration or substitution only after interviewing you. (*see §§40.135-40.145*)

There are three circumstances in which the MRO may verify a test result without an interview:

1. The MRO may verify the test result as positive or as a refusal to test, if you expressly decline the opportunity to discuss the test with the MRO. The MRO must maintain complete documentation of this.

2. The MRO may verify the test result as positive or as a refusal to test, if the DER successfully made contact with you

(instructing you to contact the MRO) and more than 72 hours have passed without you contacting the MRO.

3. The MRO may verify the test result as positive or as a refusal to test, if neither the MRO or DER (after making and documenting reasonable efforts) has been able to contact you within 10 days of the date the MRO receives the confirmed test result from the lab.

When verifying a test result as positive or refusal to test, the MRO must document the date, time, and reason.

After the MRO has verified a test result as positive or refusal to test and has reported the result to the DER, the MRO must allow you to present information within 60 days of the verification documenting that serious illness, injury, or other circumstances prevented you from contacting the MRO or DER.

On the basis of this information, the MRO may reopen the verification, allowing you to present information that could lead to a legitimate medical explanation for the confirmed test result.

§40.135 What does the MRO tell the employee at the beginning of the verification interview?

The MRO must tell you that the lab has determined that your test result was positive, adulterated, substituted, or invalid. The MRO must also tell you which drugs you tested positive for, or the basis for the finding of adulteration or substitution.

The MRO must explain the verification process to you and let you know that his/her decision will be based on the information you provide in the interview.

The MRO must also explain that if further medical evaluation is needed, you must comply with the MRO's request. Failure to do so is the same as declining to discuss the test result.

§40.137 On what basis does the MRO verify test results involving marijuana, cocaine, amphetamines, or PCP?

The MRO must verify a confirmed positive test result for marijuana, cocaine, amphetamines, and/or PCP unless you present a legitimate medical explanation for the presence of the drug(s)/metabolite(s) in your system.

The MRO must offer you an opportunity to present a legitimate medical explanation.

You have the burden of proof that a legitimate medical explanation exists, and must present information meeting this burden at the time of the verification interview.

The MRO (at his/her discretion) may allow you up to 5 additional days before verifying the test result if he/she believes you will be able to produce relevant information helping explain a medical reason for your positive test result.

If the MRO determines that there is a legitimate medical explanation, the MRO must verify the test as negative. Otherwise, the test must be verified as positive.

In determining whether a legitimate medical explanation exists, the MRO may consider your use of medication from a foreign country. The MRO must use his/her professional judgement consistently with certain principals. This includes the legality of the medication in the foreign country and the purpose of its use.

§40.139 On what basis does the MRO verify test results involving opiates?

If the lab detects the presence of 6-acetylmorphine (6-AM) in the specimen, the MRO must verify the test result as positive.

If the presence of 6-AM is not detected, but the lab detects the presence of either morphine or codeine at 15,000ng/mL or above, the MRO must verify the test as positive unless you can present a legitimate medical reason for the presence of the drug/metabolite in your system.

Consumption of food products (including poppy seeds) is *not* considered a legitimate medical explanation for having morphine or codeine at the concentration listed above.

For all other opiate-positive results, the MRO must verify a confirmed positive test result for opiates only if he/she determines there is clinical evidence, in addition to a urine test, of unauthorized use of any opium, opiate, or opium derivative.

Examples of information the MRO may consider in making his/her judgement includes, but is not limited to:

√   recent needle tracks;

√   behavioral and psychological signs of acute opiate intoxication or withdrawal;

√   clinical history of unauthorized use recent enough to have produced the lab test result; and

√   use of a medication from a foreign country (*see §40.137*).

§40.141 How does the MRO obtain information for the verification decision?

The MRO must conduct a medical interview. He/she must review your medical history and any other relevant biomedical factors you present. The MRO may direct you to undergo further medical evaluation.

If you claim that the presence of a drug or drug metabolite in your specimen is the result of taking a prescription medication, the MRO must verify the medical records you provide. The MRO may contact your physician or other relevant medical personnel for further information.

§40.145 On what basis does the MRO verify test results involving adulteration or substitution?

The MRO must treat a lab report that your specimen is adulterated or substituted the same way he/she would treat a lab report of a confirmed positive test for a drug or drug metabolite.

The MRO's procedures for verification are similar to the procedures used to verify a confirmed positive test for a drug or drug metabolite.

In the verification interview, the MRO must explain the lab's findings to you and address any technical questions you may raise.

The MRO must give you the opportunity present a legitimate medical explanation for the lab findings.

You have the burden of proof that there is a legitimate medical explanation. This information must be presented in the verification interview.

In the case of an adulterated specimen, you must demonstrate that the adulterant found by the lab entered the specimen through natural body processes (physiological means).

In the case of a substituted specimen, you must demonstrate that you did or could have produced urine through natural body processes (physiological means) that meets the criteria for creatinine concentration of less than 2 mg/dL and the specific gravity criteria of less than or equal to 1.0010 or greater than or equal to 1.0200.

The MRO (at his/her discretion) may allow you up to 5 additional days before verifying the test result if he/she believes you will be able to produce relevant information helping explain a medical reason for your test result.

Neither the MRO or your employer is responsible for arranging, conducting, or paying for any studies or examinations to determine whether a legitimate medical explanation exists.

The MRO must exercise his/her best professional judgement in deciding whether you have established a legitimate medical explanation.

If the MRO determines your explanation does not present a reasonable basis for concluding that there may be a legitimate medical explanation, the MRO must report the test to the DER as a verified refusal to test because of adulteration or substitution.

If the MRO believes your explanation may present a reasonable basis for concluding that there is a legitimate medical explanation, the MRO will direct you to obtain (within 5 days) a further medical evaluation.

This evaluation must be performed by a licensed physician with expertise in the medical issues raised by your explanation. The MRO may perform this evaluation if he/she has the appropriate expertise.

The MRO and your employer are not responsible for finding or paying for this physician. Upon your request, the MRO must provide reasonable assistance in finding such a physician.

The MRO must consult with the physician, providing guidance concerning his/her responsibilities under the regulations.

The physician must evaluate you and consider any evidence that you present concerning your medical explanation. The physician may conduct additional tests to determine whether there is a legitimate medical explanation.

The physician must make a written recommendation to the MRO as to whether the MRO should determine that there is a legitimate medical explanation. The MRO must seriously consider and assess the physician's recommendation.

If, at this point, the MRO determines there is a legitimate medical explanation, he/she must cancel the test.

If, at this point, the MRO determines there isn't a legitimate medical explanation, he/she must report the test to the DER as a verified refusal to test because of adulteration or substitution.

§40.149 May the MRO change a verified positive drug test result or refusal to test?

The MRO may change a verified positive or refusal to test result in the following situations:

1. When the MRO reopens a verification that was done without interviewing you.

2. If the MRO receives information, not available at the time of the original verification, demonstrating that the lab made an error in identifying or testing your primary or split specimen.

3. If, within 60 days of the MRO's original decision, the MRO receives information that could not reasonably have been provided at the time of the decision, demonstrating that there's a legitimate medical explanation for the presence of drug(s)/metabolite(s) in your specimen.

4. If, within 60 days of the MRO's original decision, the MRO receives credible new or additional evidence that a legitimate

medical explanation for an adulterated or substituted result exists.

5. When the MRO makes an administrative error and an incorrect result is reported.

The MRO is the only person permitted to change a verified test result. If the MRO changes the result, he/she must immediately notify the DER in writing.

§40.151 What are MROs prohibited from doing as part of the verification process?

The MRO may not consider evidence from tests of urine samples or other body fluids or tissues that are not collected or tested in accordance with Part 40.

The MRO may not make decisions about factual disputes between you and the collector concerning matters occurring at the collection site that are not noted on the CCF.

The MRO may not determine whether an employer-directed test should have occurred.

The MRO may not consider explanations that would not, even if true, constitute a legitimate medical explanation. This would include (but not be limited to) unknowingly ingesting or passively inhaling a drug.

The MRO may not verify a test negative based on information that a physician recommended that you use a drug listed in Schedule I of the Controlled Substances Act. This includes "medical marijuana" laws being used in some states.

The MRO may not consider consumption of or other use of a hemp or other non-prescription marijuana-related product as a reason for verifying a test as negative. Also, the MRO may not consider consumption of coca teas as the basis for verifying a cocaine test result as negative.

The MRO may not accept an explanation that there is a legitimate medical reason for the presence of PCP or 6-AM in a specimen, as there are no legitimate medical explanations.

The MRO may not accept as a legitimate explanation for an adulterated specimen that soap or bleach entered a specimen through natural processes (physiological means), as this isn't possible.

The MRO may not accept as a legitimate explanation for a substituted specimen that an employee can produce urine with no detectable creatinine, as this isn't possible.

§40.153 How does the MRO notify employees of their right to a test of the split specimen?

Once the MRO verifies a drug test as positive or as a refusal because of adulteration or substitution, he/she must notify you of your right to have the split specimen tested, as well as the procedures for requesting the test of the split specimen.

Additional tests of the specimen (DNA tests, etc.) are not authorized.

You have 72 hours to request the test of the split specimen. The MRO must provide telephone numbers or other information that will allow you to make this request.

If you make this request within 72 hours, your employer must ensure that the test takes place.

You are not required to pay for the test from your own funds before the test takes place, but your employer may seek reimbursement for the cost of the test.

§40.155 What does the MRO do when a negative or positive test result is also dilute?

When the lab reports that a specimen is dilute, the MRO must report to the DER that the specimen, in addition to being negative or positive, is dilute.

When reporting a dilute specimen to the DER, the MRO must explain to the DER your employer's obligations and choices (see §40.197), including the requirement for an immediate recollection under direct observation if the creatinine concentration of a negative-dilute specimen was greater than or equal to 2 mg/dL but less than or equal to 5 mg/dL.

§40.159 What does the MRO do when a drug test result is invalid?

When the lab reports that a test result is invalid, the MRO must discuss the results with a certifying scientist to get more information.

The MRO must contact you and inform you that the specimen was invalid or contained an unexplained interfering substance.

The MRO must explain the limits of disclosure to you, and will then ask if you have taken any medications that may interfere with the test.

If your explanation is acceptable the MRO must report to the DER that:

√   the test is cancelled;

√   the reason for cancellation; and

√ no further action is required unless a negative test result is required (pre-employment, return-to-duty, etc.).

If you are unable to provide an explanation and/or a valid prescription for a medication that may interfere with the test, and you deny having adulterated the specimen, the MRO must report to the DER that:

√ the test is cancelled;

√ the reason for cancellation; and

√ a second collection must take place immediately under direct observation.

If you admit to having adulterated or substituted the specimen, the MRO must, on the same day, write and sign a statement of what you told the MRO. This must be reported as a refusal to test.

§40.161 What does the MRO do when a drug test specimen is rejected for testing?

When the lab reports that your specimen is rejected for testing, the MRO must report to the DER that:

√ the test is cancelled;

√ the reason for cancellation; and

√ no further action is required unless a negative test result is required (pre-employment, return-to-duty, etc.).

§40.163 How does the MRO report drug test results?

It is the MRO's responsibility to report your drug test results to your employer.

The MRO may use a signed or stamped and dated photocopy of the CCF to report your test result. The MRO must keep a signed or stamped and dated copy of the CCF for his/her records.

If the CCF is not used to report your test result, the MRO must provide a written report containing specific information. The MRO must keep a signed or stamped and dated copy of the letter and a signed or stamped and dated copy of the CCF for his/her records.

The MRO may report negative results using an electronic data file. The electronic data file must also include specific information. A retrievable copy of this report must be kept for auditing and inspection purposes.

§40.165 To whom does the MRO transmit reports of drug test results?

The MRO must report all test results to the DER, unless your employer elects to receive reports of results through a C/TPA.

§40.167 How are MRO reports of drug results transmitted to the employer?

The MRO or C/TPA who transmits drug test results to your employer must report all results in a confidential manner.

He/she must transmit to the DER on the same day the MRO verifies the result or the next business day:

√ all verified positive test results;

√ results requiring an immediate collection under direct observation;

√ adulterated or substituted specimen results; and

√ other refusals to test.

Direct telephone contact with the DER is the preferred method of immediate reporting. The phone call must be followed up with appropriate documentation.

The MRO's written report of a verified test must be transferred to the DER so the DER receives it within 2 days of verification by the MRO.

The MRO, C/TPA, and your employer must ensure the security of the transmission and must limit access to any transmission, storage, or retrieval systems.

Only the MRO may modify or change the MRO's report.

Subpart H — Split Specimen Tests

§40.171 How does an employee request a test of a split specimen?

When the medical review officer (MRO) notifies you that you have a verified positive drug test or refusal to test because of adulteration or substitution, you have 72 hours (from the time of notification) to request a test of the split specimen.

The request may be verbal or in writing.

If you do not request a test of the split specimen within 72 hours, you may present to the MRO information documenting circumstances that prevented you from making a timely request including:

√   serious injury;

√   illness;

√   lack of notice of a verified test result; or

√   inability to contact the MRO.

If the MRO concludes that you had a legitimate reason for failing to contact the MRO within 72 hours, the MRO must direct that the test of the split specimen take place.

When you make a timely request for a test of the split specimen, the MRO must immediately notify, in writing, the lab that tested the primary specimen to forward the split specimen to a second Department of Health and Human Services (HHS)-certified lab.

The MRO must also document the date and time of your request that the split specimen be tested.

§40.173 Who is responsible for paying for the test of a split specimen?

Your employer is responsible for making sure that the MRO, and laboratories involved perform the split specimen testing in a timely manner once you have requested the test of the split specimen.

The regulations do not specify who must pay for the split specimen test as long as your employer ensures that the testing is conducted as required and the results are released appropriately.

§40.175 What steps does the first laboratory take with a split specimen?

When your primary and split specimen arrive, the lab must check to see whether the split specimen is available for testing. Because the lab is testing the primary specimen, it is not authorized to open the split specimen for any reason.

If the split specimen isn't available or is insufficient, the lab must continue the testing process on the primary specimen without any changes in the process.

If a test of the split specimen is requested by your MRO, and the split specimen isn't available or is insufficient, the lab must report to your MRO that the split specimen is unavailable for testing and explain the reason for its unavailability in as much detail as possible.

If a test of the split specimen is requested by your MRO, and the split specimen is available, the lab must forward the following to a second certified lab:

√ the split specimen in its original bottle, with seal intact;

√ a copy of the MRO's written request; and

√ a copy of the CCF (Copy 1) which identifies the drug(s) or validity criteria to be tested for.

The lab may not send to the second lab any information that could identify you.

§40.177 What does the second laboratory do with the split specimen when it is tested to reconfirm the presence of a drug or drug metabolite?

The lab testing the split specimen must test for the drug(s) detected in the primary specimen. This test must be conducted without regard to cutoff concentrations.

If the test fails to reconfirm the presence of the drug(s) that were reported positive in the primary specimen, validity tests must be conducted in an attempt to determine the reason for being unable to reconfirm the presence of the drug(s). Also, the specimen may be transmitted to another lab for another reconfirmation test.

§40.179 What does the second laboratory do with the split specimen when it is tested to reconfirm an adulterated test result?

The lab testing the split specimen must test for the adulterant detected in the primary specimen using the same criteria as the previous test.

The result of the primary specimen is reconfirmed if the split specimen meets these criteria.

§40.181 What does the second laboratory do with the split specimen when it is tested to reconfirm a substituted test result?

The lab testing the split specimen must test the primary specimen using the same criteria as the previous test.

The result of the primary specimen is reconfirmed if the split specimen meets these criteria.

§40.183 What information do laboratories report to MROs regarding split specimen results?

The lab responsible for testing the split specimen must report the test results by checking the "Reconfirmed" box or "Failed to Reconfirm" box on the CCF.

If the "Failed to Reconfirm" box is checked, the reason for this result must be stated and the certifying scientist must sign and date the CCF.

§40.185 Through what methods and to whom must a laboratory report split specimen results?

The lab testing the split specimen results must report the lab results directly, and only, to the MRO at his/her place of business. This transmission should occur on the same day or next business day as the result is released.

§40.187 What does the MRO do with split specimen laboratory results?

In the case of a reconfirmed positive drug test result, the MRO must report the reconfirmation to you and your company's DER.

In the case of a reconfirmed adulterated or substituted test result, the MRO must report the reconfirmation to you and your company's DER. An adulterated or substituted test constitutes a refusal to test and is reported as such.

In the case of a reconfirmed substituted result, in which the creatinine concentration for the primary specimen was less than 2 mg/dL and the creatinine concentration of the split specimen is between 2 and 5 mg/dL, inclusive, the MRO must report the result to your company's DER as "dilute." The MRO will then instruct the DER to conduct an immediate recollection under direct observation.

In the case of failure to reconfirm a positive, adulterated, or substituted test result, the MRO must report the cancellation of both the primary and split specimen test to you and your company's DER.

In the case of failure to reconfirm because the split specimen was not available for testing, the MRO must report the cancellation of both the primary and split specimen test to you and your company's DER and the reason for the cancellation. The MRO will then instruct the DER to ensure the immediate collection of another specimen from you under direct observation. You will be given no advance notice of this collection.

In the case of failure to reconfirm because the specimen results were invalid, the MRO must report the cancellation of both tests to you and your company's DER and the reason for the cancellation. The MRO will then instruct the DER to ensure the immediate collection of another specimen under direct observation. You will be given no advance notice of this collection.

In the case of failure to reconfirm because the split specimen was adulterated, the MRO must inform you that the lab has determined your split specimen is adulterated. The MRO will then follow certain procedures to determine whether there is a medical explanation for the lab's finding. (*see §40.145*)

If the MRO determines that there is a legitimate medical explanation for the adulterated test result, the MRO will report to you and the DER that the test is cancelled.

If the MRO determines that there is not a legitimate medical explanation for the adulterated test result, the MRO must report to you and the DER that the test result is a verified refusal to test. You will then have 72 hours to request a test of the primary specimen to determine if the adulterant found in the split specimen is also present in the primary specimen.

If the test of the primary specimen reconfirms the adulteration finding of the split specimen, the MRO must report the test result as a refusal.

If the test of the primary specimen fails to re-confirm the adulteration finding of the split specimen, the MRO must cancel the test.

Subpart I — Problems in Drug Tests

§40.191 What is a refusal to take a DOT drug test, and what are the consequences?

You have refused to take a drug test if you:

√   fail to appear for any test (except a pre-employment test) within a reasonable time, as determined by your employer;

√   fail to remain at the testing site until the testing process is complete (except leaving the testing site before the pre-employment testing process begins);

√   fail to provide a urine specimen for a drug test required by the regulations (except when a specimen is not provided due to leaving the testing site before the pre-employment testing process begins);

√   don't allow the observation or monitoring of a collection that, according to the regulations, must be directly observed or monitored;

√ fail to provide a sufficient amount of urine when directed when there is no adequate explanation of the failure;

√ fail or decline taking an additional drug test as directed by your employer or the collector;

√ fail to undergo a medical examination or evaluation, as directed by the medical review officer (MRO) as part of the verification process, or as directed by the designated employer representative (DER) as part of "shy bladder" procedures (In the case of a pre-employment test, this is considered a refusal only when the test is conducted following a contingent offer of employment. If there was no contingent offer of employment, the MRO will cancel the test.); or

√ fail to cooperate with any part of the testing process.

If the MRO reports that you have a verified adulterated or substituted test result, you have refused to take a drug test.

If you refuse to participate in the testing process, the MRO or collector must:

√ terminate the testing process;

√ document the refusal on the custody and control form (CCF); and

√ immediately notify the DER.

There are no consequences under DOT regulations for refusing to take a non-DOT test.

§40.193 What happens when an employee does not provide a sufficient amount of urine for a drug test?

If you can't provide a sufficient amount of urine (at least 45mL) the collector must discard the specimen (unless it shows signs of adulteration or tampering).

The collector will urge you to drink up to 40 ounces of fluid, distributed through a period of up to 3 hours, or until you have provided a sufficient specimen, whichever occurs first. (*Note:* It is not considered a refusal to test if you refuse to drink the fluid.)

Refusing to make the second attempt to provide a urine specimen or leaving the collection site before the collection process is complete is considered a refusal to test.

If you do not provide a sufficient specimen within 3 hours of the first unsuccessful attempt, the collector must discontinue the collection, note this on the CCF, and notify the DER.

After consulting with the MRO, the DER will direct you to obtain an evaluation from a licensed physician. The physician must be acceptable to the MRO and must have expertise in medical issues raised by your failure to provide a sufficient specimen. The MRO may perform the evaluation if he/she has appropriate expertise. The evaluation must take place within 5 days.

The physician conducting the evaluation will recommend that the MRO make one of the following determinations:

1. A medical condition could have prevented you from providing a sufficient amount of urine. If this is the case, the test must be cancelled.

2. There isn't enough information to prove that a medical condition could have prevented you from providing a sufficient amount of urine for testing. If this is the case, this is a refusal to test.

§40.195 What happens when an individual is unable to provide a sufficient amount of urine for a pre-employment, follow-up, or return-to-duty test because of a permanent or long-term medical condition?

If you have a medical condition that prevents you from providing a sufficient specimen, and it is considered a permanent or long-term disability, the MRO (or a physician acceptable to the MRO) must determine if there is clinical evidence that you are a drug user. Evidence is gathered by:

√ medical evaluation; and

√ consultation with your physician.

An alternative test (blood test) may be done as part of the medical evaluation.

If this evaluation shows no clinical evidence of drug use, this must be reported as a negative test.

If this evaluation shows clinical evidence of drug use, this must be reported as a cancelled test.

§40.197 What happens when an employer receives a report of a dilute specimen?

If the MRO reports to your employer that your positive drug test was dilute, it must be treated as a verified positive test. Your employer can't direct you to take a new test.

If the MRO reports to your employer that your negative drug test was dilute, your employer must take the following action:

1. If the MRO directs your employer to conduct a recollection under direct observation, your employer must do so immediately.

2. Otherwise, your employer may, but is not required to, direct you to take another test immediately.

   Such recollections must not be done under direct observation unless there is another basis for use of direct observation.

   Your employer must treat all employees the same. (For example, your employer may not retest some employees and not others.) However, your employer may establish different policies for different types of tests. You must be informed (in advance) of these policies.

If you are directed to take another test you will be give as little advance notice as possible.

The second test will be considered the test of record.

If the second test is negative and dilute, your employer may not direct you to take an additional test unless the MRO directs your employer to do so.

If you refuse to take a second test, this is considered a refusal, which is then treated the same as a positive test.

§40.199 What problems always cause a drug test to be cancelled?

When the laboratory discovers a "fatal flaw" the specimen is rejected for testing. This is reported by the lab to the MRO.

The following are "fatal flaws":

√ there is no printed collector's name and no collector's signature;

√ the specimen ID numbers on the specimen bottle and CCF do not match;

√ the specimen bottle seal is broken or shows evidence of tampering (and the split specimen cannot be tested); and

√ because of leakage or other causes, there is an insufficient amount of urine in the primary bottle (and the split specimen cannot be tested).

§40.201 What problems always cause a drug test to be cancelled and may result in the requirement for another collection?

The MRO must cancel a drug test when a lab reports any of the following problems:

√ an "invalid result";

√ a specimen "rejected for testing";

√ the laboratory's test of the primary specimen is positive and the split specimen is reported as "failure to reconfirm: drug(s)/drug metabolite(s) not detected;"

√ the laboratory's test of the primary specimen is adulterated or substituted and the split specimen is reported as "adulterant not found within criteria" or "specimen not consistent with substitution criteria";

√ the laboratory's test of the primary specimen if positive, adulterated, or substituted and the split specimen is unavailable for testing; or

√ the examining physician has determined there is an acceptable medical explanation for failure to provide a sufficient amount of urine.

§40.207 What is the effect of a cancelled drug test?

A cancelled drug test is neither positive nor negative.

Your employer may not remove you from safety-sensitive functions or treat you as if you tested positive.

A cancelled test may not be considered a negative test for the purposes of a pre-employment, return-to-duty, or follow-up test.

A cancelled test does not count toward meeting DOT requirements for conducting a specific amount of tests.

A cancelled test does not provide a valid basis for an employer to conduct a non-DOT test.

§40.208 What problem requires corrective action but does not result in the cancellation of a test?

No one in the testing process may cancel a test because the specimen temperature on the CCF was not checked and there wasn't an entry regarding the temperature being out of range. In this case, corrective action must be taken. This includes securing a memo explaining the problem.

§40.209 What procedural problems do not result in the cancellation of a test and do not require correction?

No one involved in the testing process may cancel a test based on an error that doesn't have a significant adverse effect on your right to have a fair and accurate test. This includes:

√   a minor administrative mistake;

√   an error that doesn't affect employee protections;

√   collection of a specimen by a collector who has not met the training requirement (*see §40.33*);

√   a delay in the collection process;

√   verification of a test result by an MRO who has the basic credentials to be qualified, but who hasn't met the training or documentation requirements (*see §40.121*);

√   failure to directly observe or monitor a collection or unauthorized use of direct observation or monitoring of a collection;

√ the fact a test was conducted in a facility that does not meet the testing requirements (*see §40.41*);

√ the specific name of the courier is omitted from the CCF;

√ personal identifying information is mistakenly placed on the CCF; or

√ claims that someone was improperly selected for testing.

Even though these types of errors are not enough to cancel a drug test result, your employer or the service agent involved may be subject to enforcement action under DOT regulations. (*see Part 40, Subpart R*)

Subpart J — Alcohol Testing Personnel

§40.211 Who conducts DOT alcohol tests?

Screening test technicians (STTs) and breath alcohol technicians (BATs) are the only people authorized to conduct Department of Transportation (DOT) alcohol tests.

An STT can only conduct alcohol screening tests. A BAT can conduct alcohol screening and confirmation tests.

If your supervisor is a qualified BAT or STT he/she may not act as the BAT or STT when you are tested, unless no other BAT or STT is available and DOT regulations do not prohibit the supervisor from doing the testing.

§40.213 What training requirements must STTs and BATs meet?

A BAT or STT must be knowledgeable about the Part 40 alcohol testing procedures.

He/she must receive training in accordance with the DOT Model BAT or STT Course, as applicable.

The training must include training to proficiency in the Part 40 alcohol testing procedures and in the operation of the alcohol testing device(s) he/she will be using.

The training must emphasize the integrity of the process and the privacy of those being tested.

Following completion of the qualification training, the BAT must complete seven error-free mock tests using the device(s) the BAT will be using. Following completion of the qualification training, the STT must complete five consecutive error-free tests using the deceive(s) the STT will be using.

Each BAT or STT must complete refresher training at least once every 5 years.

If a BAT or STT makes a mistake in the alcohol testing process that causes a test to be cancelled, he/she must undergo correction training within 30 days.

Each BAT or STT must maintain evidence of his/her qualifications and must be able to provide it on request to the DOT or your employer.

Law enforcement officers who have been certified by state or local government to conduct breath alcohol testing are also qualified as BATs.

Subpart K — Testing Sites, Forms, Equipment and Supplies Used in Alcohol Testing

§40.221 Where does an alcohol test take place?

Alcohol testing must take place at a site that provides privacy — enough to prevent unauthorized persons from seeing or hearing your test results.

The site must have all needed personnel, materials, equipment, and facilities, including a suitable clean surface for writing.

Reasonable suspicion and post-accident tests may be conducted at a site that partially meets the requirements if an alcohol testing site fully meeting all of the requirements isn't available. The site must provide as much privacy as possible.

A testing site can be:

√ a medical facility;

√ a mobile facility;

√ a dedicated collection facility; or

√ any other location meeting the requirements.

§40.223 What steps must be taken to protect the security of alcohol testing sites?

Only authorized persons are allowed to enter the testing site. This includes:

√ individuals being tested;

√ breath alcohol technicians (BATs), screening test technicians (STTs), and other alcohol testing site workers;

√ designated employer representatives (DERs);

√ employee representatives authorized by your employer; and

√ Department of Transportation (DOT) agency representatives.

Only you, the BAT or STT, or a DOT agency representative may actually watch the testing process.

When not in use, the evidential breath testing device (EBT) or alcohol screening device (ASD) must be stored in a secure place. When unsecured, only the BAT, STT, or other site employees may have access to the device.

For security reasons, the BAT or STT may only conduct one alcohol test at a time.

When an EBT screening test indicates an alcohol concentration of 0.02 or higher, and the same EBT is used for the confirmation test, the EBT may not be used for a test on another person before the confirmation test is completed.

The BAT must complete both the screening and confirmation test on one person before starting the screening process on another person.

He/she may not leave the testing site while the testing is in progress, except to contact a DER for help in the case of a person who interferes, obstructs, or delays the testing process.

§40.225 What form is used for an alcohol test?

As of February 1, 2002, the DOT Alcohol Testing Form (ATF) must be used. The ATF is a three-part carbonless manifold form.

The ATF may not be revised or modified. There are a few exceptions to this requirement. These include placing billing information on the outside boundaries of the form and preprinting the employer's company information.

An ATF generated directly by an EBT which omits the space for attaching a separate printed result to the ATF, provided the EBT prints the result directly on the ATF, may also be used.

An equivalent foreign-language version of the form may be used if the BAT or STT and person being tested understand and can use the form in that language.

§40.227 May employers use the ATF for non-DOT tests, or non-DOT forms for DOT tests?

No. Using the ATF for a non-DOT test or using non-DOT forms for a DOT test is prohibited. Doing either subjects your employer and the BAT or STT to enforcement action under DOT regulations.

If the BAT or STT either by mistake, or as the only means to conduct a test under difficult circumstances, uses a non-DOT form for a DOT test, the use of the non-DOT form doesn't require the employer or a service agent to cancel the test. For the test to be considered valid, the BAT or STT must provide a signed statement.

§40.229 What devices are used to conduct alcohol screening tests?

Only EBTs and ASDs on the National Highway Transportation Safety Administration (NHTSA) conforming products list (CPL) may be used. Only ASDs with instructions for use that are covered in Part 40 may be used. An ASD may only be used for screening tests. An ASD may not be used for confirmation tests.

§40.231 What devices are used to conduct alcohol confirmation tests?

Only EBTs on the NHTSA CPL for evidential devices may be used to conduct alcohol confirmation tests.

The EBT must be able to perform several tasks including the printing of specific information on the test result, the testing of an air blank, and an external calibration check.

§40.233 What are the requirements for proper use and care of EBTs?

An EBT manufacturer must have a quality assurance plan and must include with each EBT instructions for its use and care.

The user of the EBT must follow the manufacturer's instructions and perform external calibration checks.

If an EBT fails an external calibration check, it must be taken out of service and may not be used again until it's repaired and passes an external calibration check.

The user of the EBT must maintain records of inspection, maintenance, and calibration.

§40.235 What are the requirements for proper use and care of ASDs?

An ASD manufacturer must have a quality assurance plan and must include with each ASD instructions for its use and care. These instructions must include:

√ directions on the proper use of the ASD; and

√ (where applicable) the time within which the device must be read, and the manner in which the reading is made.

An ASD that doesn't pass specified quality control checks or has passed the expiration date may not be used.

Subpart L — Alcohol Screening Tests

§40.241 What are the first steps in any alcohol screening test?

The breath alcohol technician (BAT) or screening test technician (STT) must take the following steps before beginning an alcohol screening test:

1. If a specific time has been scheduled for your test or the testing site is your work-

site, and you do not appear there at the scheduled time, the designated employer representative (DER) will be contacted to determine what time period is acceptable for your arrival. If your arrival is delayed beyond that time, the BAT or STT must notify the DER.

In the case where a consortium/third party administrator (C/TPA) has notified an owner-operator or other employee to report for testing and he/she does not appear, the C/TPA must notify the employee that he/she has refused to test.

2. Once you enter the alcohol testing site, the testing process must begin without delay.

   If you are taking both the alcohol and drug test, if at all possible, the alcohol test must be completed before the drug test begins.

   If you need medical attention, treatment should not be delayed in order to complete an alcohol test.

3. You must provide positive identification. This includes, but is not limited to, a com-

pany issued photo ID or a driver's license. Faxes or photocopies are not acceptable. Positive identification by your employer is also acceptable.

4. You may ask the BAT or STT for identification as well.

5. The BAT or STT must explain the basic collection procedure to you, including showing you the instructions on the back of the alcohol testing form (ATF).

6. You will be directed to complete and sign Step 2 on the ATF. Refusing to do this is considered a refusal to test.

§40.243 What is the procedure for an alcohol screening test using an EBT or non-evidential breath ASD?

The procedure for an alcohol screening test is as follows:

1. The BAT or STT will select or allow you to select an individually wrapped or sealed mouthpiece.

2. The BAT or STT will open the individually wrapped or sealed mouthpiece in front

of you and insert the mouthpiece into the device.

3. You will be instructed to blow steadily and forcefully for at least 6 seconds or until the device indicates that an adequate amount of breath has been obtained.

4. You will be shown the displayed test result.

5. If the device prints the results on a separate document rather than on the ATF, the printout must be affixed to the ATF with tamper-evident tape or a self-adhesive label that is tamper-evident.

6. If the device doesn't print the results, the BAT or STT must record the information on the ATF.

§40.245 What is the procedure for an alcohol screening test using a saliva ASD or a breath tube ASD?

The procedure for an alcohol saliva screening test is as follows:

1. The STT must check the device's expiration date and show it to you. A device may not be used after its expiration date.

2. The STT will open an individually wrapped or sealed package containing the device in front of you.

3. You will be asked to place the device in your mouth and use it in the manner described by the device's manufacturer.

4. If you decline to use the device, or in a case where the device doesn't activate, the STT must insert the device in your mouth and use it in the manner described by the device's manufacturer. The STT must wear single-use examination gloves and must change the gloves following each test.

5. When the device is removed from your mouth, the STT must follow the manufacturer's instructions to ensure the device is activated.

6. If the procedures listed above can't be successfully completed, the device must be discarded and a new test must be conducted using a new device.

7. Again, you will be offered the choice of using the new device or having the STT use the device for your test.

8. If the new test can't be successfully completed, you will be directed to immediately take a screening test using an EBT.

The result displayed on the device must be read within 15 minutes of the test. The STT must show you the device and its reading and enter the result on the ATF.

The materials used in saliva testing (devices, swabs, gloves) must never be reused.

The procedure for an alcohol breath tube screening test is as follows:

1. The STT must check the expiration date on the detector device and the electronic analyzer or on the package containing the device and the analyzer and show it to you. A device or analyzer must not be used after their expiration date. The STT must not use an analyzer which is not specifically precalibrated for the device being used in the collection.

2. The STT will remove the device from the package and secure an inflation bag onto the appropriate end of the device.

3. The STT will break the tube's ampoule in front of you.

4. You will be asked to use the device and blow forcefully and steadily into it until

the inflation bag fills with air (approximately 12 seconds). If you decline to use the device, the STT will hold it and instruct you about what to do.

5. When you complete the breath process, the STT will take the device from you (or if you were holding it, the STT will remove it from your mouth), remove the inflation bag, and prepare the device to be read by the analyzer.

6. If the procedures listed above can't be successfully completed, the device must be discarded and a new test must be conducted using a new device.

7. If the new test can't be successfully completed, you will be directed to immediately take a screening test using a different type of screening device or an EBT.

8. If the screening test is successfully completed, and after having waited the required amount of time for the detector device to incubate, the STT must place the device in the analyzer. The result must be read from the analyzer no earlier than the required incubation time of the device. In all cases, the result must be read within 15 minutes of the test.

9. The STT must follow the manufacturer's instructions for determining the result of the test. The STT must show the analyzer result to you and record the result on the ATF.

10. The STT must never reuse detector devices or any gloves used in breath tube testing. The inflation bag must be voided of air following removal from a device. Inflation bags and electronic analyzers may be reused but only in accordance with the manufacturer's directions.

§40.247 What procedures does the BAT or STT follow after a screening test result?

If the test result is an alcohol concentration of less than 0.02 the BAT or STT must:

√ sign and date the ATF; and

√ transmit the results to the DER in a confidential manner.

If the test result is an alcohol concentration of 0.02 or higher the BAT or STT will direct you to take a confirmation test.

If the BAT who conducted the screening test will conduct the confirmation test the procedures in Part 40, Subpart M will be used.

If the BAT who conducted the screening test will not conduct the confirmation test, he/she will direct you to take a confirmation test, sign and date the ATF, and give you one of the copies.

If the confirmation test will be performed at a different site from the screening test, you will be observed by the BAT, another BAT or STT, or a company representative. You may not drive yourself to the confirmation testing site.

You will be advised to not eat, drink, belch, or put anything into your mouth.

You will be told why there is a waiting period prior to the confirmation test.

Even if you do not follow the instructions, a confirmation test will be given.

If the screening test is invalid, the BAT or STT will tell you the test is cancelled, and the testing process should be repeated.

Subpart M — Alcohol Confirmation Tests

§40.251 What are the first steps in an alcohol confirmation test?

The breath alcohol technician (BAT) conducting the alcohol confirmation test must make sure the waiting period is at least 15 minutes, but is no longer than 30 minutes. The waiting period starts when the screening test is finished.

The BAT or another BAT or screening test technician (STT) must be with you for the entire waiting period.

You will be told not to eat, drink, put anything into your mouth, or belch. This is to prevent a build-up of mouth alcohol, which could lead to a false high alcohol reading. Even if you don't follow the BAT's directions, the confirmation test will be conducted.

If the BAT conducting the confirmation test did not perform the screening test, you will be asked for identification, the BAT will explain the procedure, and a new alcohol testing form (ATF) will be used.

Even if more than 30 minutes have passed since the screening test, the confirmation test must be conducted.

The BAT will state the reason for the delay on the ATF.

A delay of more than 30 minutes does not invalidate the test, but may constitute a violation of the regulations.

§40.253 What are the procedures for conducting an alcohol confirmation test?

The BAT must follow the following steps when conducting an alcohol confirmation test:

1. The BAT must conduct an air blank on the evidential breath testing device (EBT) and show you the reading. If the reading is 0.00 the test will begin.

   If the reading is greater than 0.00 a second test must be conducted and you must be shown the reading. If the reading for the second test is 0.00 the test may proceed. If it is greater than 0.00 the EBT must not be used and another EBT must be used.

2. The BAT will open a new individually sealed mouthpiece in front of you and insert it into the EBT.

3. Both you and the BAT must read the test number displayed on the EBT.

4. The BAT will tell you to blow forcefully into the mouthpiece for at least 6 seconds or until the device indicates an adequate amount of breath.

5. The BAT will show you the result on the EBT.

6. You will then be shown the result as printed either directly onto the ATF or onto a separate printout.

7. If the result is printed onto a separate printout it must be placed on the ATF with tamper-evident tape.

§40.255 What happens next after the alcohol confirmation test result?

After the EBT has printed the result, the BAT will sign and date the ATF.

If the result is less than 0.02 nothing further is required.

If the result of the confirmation test is 0.02 or higher, you will be asked to sign and date the ATF.

If the test is invalid, you will be told the test is cancelled. If possible, a retest will be conducted. (see §40.271)

All results must be immediately sent to the designated employer representative (DER) in a confidential manner.

If the result of the confirmation test is 0.02 or higher, the BAT must ensure that the DER receives the result immediately (telephone, secure fax). This result cannot be transmitted through a service agent.

If the initial transmission is not in writing, a copy of the ATF must be sent as a follow-up.

If your employer receives test results that are not in writing, your employer must have a way to positively identify the BAT sending the results and must have a way to store the results that ensures confidentiality.

Subpart N — Problems in Alcohol Testing

§40.261 What is a refusal to take an alcohol test, and what are the consequences?

You have refused to take an alcohol test if you:

√ fail to appear for any test (except a pre-employment test) within a reasonable time, as determined by your employer;

√ fail to remain at the testing site until the testing process is complete (except leaving the testing site before the pre-employment testing process begins);

√ fail to provide a saliva or breath specimen (as applicable) for an alcohol test required by the regulations (except when a saliva or breath specimen is not provided due to leaving the testing site before the pre-employment testing process begins);

√ fail to provide a sufficient amount of breath specimen when directed and there is no adequate medical explanation of the failure;

√ fail to undergo a medical examination or evaluation, as directed by your employer as part of insufficient breath procedures;

√ fail to sign the alcohol testing form (ATF); or

√ fail to cooperate with any part of the testing process.

If you refuse to take an alcohol test, you are subject to the same consequences as if you failed an alcohol test.

The breath alcohol technician (BAT), screening test technician (STT), or physician evaluating you in the case of "shy lung" will document the refusal on the ATF and will immediately notify the designated employer representative (DER).

There are no consequences under Department of Transportation (DOT) regulations for refusing to take a non-DOT test.

§40.263 What happens when an employee is unable to provide a sufficient amount of saliva for an alcohol screening test?

If you can't provide a sufficient amount of saliva, the STT must conduct a new screening test using a new screening device.

If you refuse to make an attempt to complete a new test this will be considered a refusal to test. The test will be stopped, the result recorded on the ATF, and the DER will be notified.

If you can't provide enough saliva to complete the new test, an evidential breath testing device (EBT) will be used to complete the test.

§40.265 What happens when an employee is unable to provide a sufficient amount of breath for an alcohol test?

If you can't provide a sufficient amount of breath, the BAT or STT will ask you to try again.

If you refuse to make the attempt, this is considered a refusal to test. This will be recorded on the ATF and the DER will be notified.

If you again attempt and fail to provide a sufficient amount of breath, the BAT or STT may ask you to try a third time.

If, at that point, you can't provide a sufficient amount of breath, this will be recorded on the ATF and the DER will be notified.

If the EBT can be operated manually, the BAT or STT may conduct the test in the manual mode.

If this is a screening test, and the BAT or STT is qualified to use an alcohol screening device (ASD), this may be used instead of a breath testing device.

If you cannot provide a sufficient amount of breath your employer will direct you to obtain a medical evaluation within 5 days.

The evaluation must be done by a licensed physician who has expertise in the medical issues raised by your failure to provide a sufficient specimen.

After the evaluation, the physician must provide a signed statement of his/her conclusions. The physician must base his/her conclusions on the following determinations:

1. A medical condition has, or with a high degree of probability, could have prevented you from providing a sufficient amount of breath. Additional medical information may not be included in the physician's signed statement.

   In this case the test is cancelled.

2. There is not an adequate basis for determining that a medical condition has, or with a high degree of probability, could have prevented you from providing a sufficient amount of breath.

   This is considered a refusal to test

After making his/her determination, the physician must provide a written statement of his/her conclusions and the basis for them to the DER.

This statement must not include detailed information on your medical condition beyond what is necessary to explain the physician's conclusion.

Upon receipt of the report, the DER must immediately notify you and take appropriate actions.

§40.267 What problems always cause an alcohol test to be cancelled?

Your employer, a BAT, or STT must cancel a screening test conducted on a saliva or breath tube ASD if any of the following "fatal flaws" occur:

√   the STT reads the result either sooner or later than the time allotted by the manufacturer;

√   the device does not activate;

√   the device is used for a test after the expiration date printed on its package; or

√ the breath tube ASD is tested with an analyzer which has not been precalibrated for the device's specific lot.

Your employer, a BAT, or STT must cancel a screening or confirmation test conducted on an EBT if the test number or alcohol concentration displayed on the EBT is not the same as the printed result.

Your employer or the BAT must cancel a confirmation test if any of the following "fatal flaws" occur:

√ the BAT conducts the confirmation test before the end of the minimum 15 minute waiting period;

√ the BAT does not conduct an air blank before the confirmation test;

√ there is not a 0.00 result on the air blank conducted before the confirmation test;

√ the EBT doesn't print the result; or

√ the next external calibration check of the EBT produces a result that doesn't meet the testing standards (*see §40.233*).

§40.269 What problems cause an alcohol test to be cancelled unless they are corrected?

Your employer, a BAT, or STT must cancel an alcohol test if any of the following problems occur and they are not corrected. "Correctable flaws" include the following:

√ the BAT or STT doesn't sign the ATF;

√ the BAT or STT fails to note on the ATF that you have not signed the ATF after the result is obtained; or

√ the BAT or STT uses a non-DOT form for the test.

§40.271 How are alcohol testing problems corrected?

The BAT or STT has the responsibility of trying to successfully complete each alcohol test.

If, shortly after the testing process, the BAT or STT becomes aware of something that will cause a test to be cancelled, he/she must try to correct the problem promptly. The testing process may be repeated as part of the correction effort.

If repeating the testing process is necessary, the BAT or STT must begin a new test as soon as possible. A new ATF, test number, and if needed, a new ASD and/or a new EBT must be used.

If repeating the testing process is necessary, the BAT or STT is not limited in the number of attempts to complete a test, provided you are making a good faith effort to comply with the testing process.

If another testing device is not available for a new test at the testing site, the BAT or STT must notify the DER. The DER must make all reasonable efforts to ensure that the test is conducted at another testing site as soon as possible.

If the STT, BAT, your employer, or other service agent administering the testing process becomes aware of a "correctable flaw," he/she must take action (if practicable) to correct the flaw so the test is not cancelled.

If the problem resulted from the omission of required information, the person responsible for providing that information must supply, in writing, the missing information and a signed statement that it is true and accurate.

If the problem is the use of a non-DOT form, the person responsible for the use of the incorrect form must certify, in writing, that the incorrect form contains all the information needed for a valid DOT alcohol test.

He/she must also provide a signed statement that the incorrect form was used by mistake or as the only means to conduct a test under circumstances beyond his/her control and that steps have been taken to prevent future use of non-DOT forms for DOT tests.

If the problem can't be corrected the test must be cancelled.

§40.273 What is the effect of a cancelled alcohol test?

A cancelled alcohol test is neither positive nor negative.

Your employer may not treat a cancelled test the same way as an alcohol test with a result of 0.02 or greater. You may not be removed from a safety-sensitive position.

Your employer may not use a cancelled test in a situation where you need a test result that is below 0.02.

Your employer may not direct a recollection because your test has been cancelled, except in specific situations addressed in Part 40.

A cancelled test does not count toward the minimum random testing rate.

The BAT or STT must inform the DER of a cancelled test within 48 hours.

A cancelled DOT test is not a valid reason for your employer to conduct a non-DOT test.

§40.275 What is the effect of procedural problems that are not sufficient to cancel an alcohol test?

Your employer, an STT, or BAT administering the testing process must document any errors in the testing process, even if they are not "fatal flaws" or "correctable flaws."

No one involved in the testing process may cancel a test based on a mistake that does not have a significant adverse effect on your right to a fair and accurate test.

Though these errors may not result in a cancelled test, your employer may be subject to enforcement action under DOT regulations.

§40.277 Are alcohol tests other than saliva or breath permitted under these regulations?

No. Other types of alcohol tests (blood, urine, etc.) are not authorized for Part 40 testing. Only saliva or breath screening tests and breath for confirmation tests using approved devices are permitted.

Subpart O — Substance Abuse Professionals and the Return-to-Duty Process

§40.281 Who is qualified to act as a SAP?

An individual must have certain credentials, knowledge, and training to act as a substance abuse professional (SAP). He/she must be a:

√   licensed physician (Doctor of Medicine or Osteopathy);

√   licensed or certified social worker;

√   licensed or certified psychologist;

√   licensed or certified employee assistance professional;

√   state-licensed or certified marriage and family therapist; or

√   a drug and alcohol counselor certified by the National Association of Alcoholism and Drug Abuse Counselors Certification Commission (NAADAC); or by the International Certification Reciprocity Consortium/Alcohol and Other Drug Abuse (ICRC); or by the National Board for Certified Counselors, Inc. and Affiliates/Master Addictions Counselor (NBCC).

To act as a SAP an individual must have knowledge and clinical experience in the diagnosis and treatment of alcohol and controlled substances-related disorders.

He/she must know the Part 40 regulations, other applicable Department of Transportation (DOT) agency regulations, and the DOT's SAP Guidelines.

The SAP must receive qualification training and must pass an exam given by a nationally-recognized professional or training organization.

After passing the exam, the SAP is required to complete 12 professional development hours related to performing SAP functions once every 3 years.

The SAP must keep all documentation showing he/she meets the requirements. This information must be available upon request to DOT agency representatives, your employer, and consortium/third party administrators (C/TPAs) who are using or considering using the SAP's services.

§40.285 When is a SAP evaluation required?

When you have violated DOT drug and alcohol regulations (alcohol concentration of 0.04 or greater, refusal to test, or failing a drug test) you can't perform safety-sensitive functions for any employer until you complete the SAP evaluation, referral, and education/treatment process. The first step is a SAP evaluation.

§40.287 What information is an employer required to provide concerning SAP services to an employee who has a DOT drug and alcohol regulation violation?

If you violate a DOT drug or alcohol regulation, your employer must provide, free of charge, a list of SAPs. The list must include SAP names, addresses, and telephone numbers. This list may be provided by your employer or through a consortium/third party administrator (C/TPA).

§40.289 Are employers required to provide SAP and treatment services to employees?

Your employer is not required to provide a SAP evaluation or any recommended education or treatment.

However, if your employer offers you an opportunity to return to a safety-sensitive function following a violation, your employer must make sure you received a SAP evaluation and you successfully complied with the SAP's recommendations.

The regulation does not address who should pay for SAP evaluations. It is left to you and your employer to decide on payment.

§40.291 What is the role of the SAP in the evaluation, referral, and treatment process of an employee who has violated DOT agency drug and alcohol testing regulations?

The SAP must:

1. Make a face-to-face clinical assessment and evaluation to determine what assistance is needed to resolve your problems with alcohol and/or drug use.

2. Refer you to an appropriate education and/or treatment program.

3. Conduct face-to-face follow-up evaluation to determine if you actively participated in the education and/or treatment program and if you demonstrate successful compliance with the initial assessment and evaluation recommendations.

4. Provide the designated employer representative (DER) with your follow-up drug and/or alcohol testing plan.

5. Provide you and your employer with rec-
    ommendations for continuing education
    and/or treatment.

The SAP is not an advocate for either you or
your employer. His/her job is to protect public
interest in safety by professionally evaluating
you and recommending appropriate education,
treatment, follow-up tests, and aftercare.

§40.293 What is the SAP's function in conducting the initial evaluation of an employee?

When you go to a SAP he/she must:

√ provide a comprehensive face-to-face assessment and clinical evaluation;

√ recommend a course of education and/or
  treatment that you must successfully
  comply with before returning to safety-
  sensitive functions; and

√ provide a written report to the DER listing his/her recommendations.

The SAP must assume that a verified positive test result means you violated a DOT
drug or alcohol regulation. The SAP must not
take into consideration any of the following
as a factor in determining his/her recommended treatment:

√ a claim (by you) that the test was unjustified or inaccurate;

√ statements (by you) that attempt to reduce the seriousness of a violation of a DOT drug and/or alcohol regulation;

√ personal opinions the SAP may have about the justification or rationale for drug and alcohol testing.

When gathering information as part of the evaluation process, the SAP may consult with the medical review officer (MRO). The MRO may provide information to the SAP without your consent.

§40.295 May employees or employers seek a second SAP evaluation if they disagree with the first SAP's recommendations?

No. After you have been evaluated by a SAP, you or your employer may not seek a second SAP's evaluation.

If you obtain a second SAP evaluation, your employer may not accept it for any purpose.

§40.297 Does anyone have the authority to change a SAP's initial evaluation?

Only the SAP who made the initial evaluation may modify his/her initial evaluation and recommendation based on new or additional information. No one else may change, in any way, the SAP's evaluation or recommendation.

§40.299 What is the SAP's role and what are the limits on a SAP's discretion in referring employees for education and treatment?

Once the SAP has determined what assistance is needed, he/she will serve as a referral source, helping you start an education and/or treatment program.

To prevent the appearance of a conflict of interest, the SAP can't refer you to his/her private practice or to a person or organization from which the SAP receives payment or has a financial interest.

You may be referred to the following assistance providers regardless of the SAP's relationship with them:

√ a public agency operated by a state, county, or municipality;

√ a person or organization under contract to your employer to provide treatment and/or education services;

√   the only source of appropriate treatment under your health insurance program; or

√   the only source of treatment reasonably available to you.

§40.301 What is the SAP's function in the follow-up evaluation of an employee?

The SAP who prescribed assistance must re-evaluate you to determine if you successfully carried out his/her education and/or treatment recommendations.

The SAP making the follow-up evaluation must:

√   confer with or obtain appropriate documentation from the education and/or treatment programs where you were referred; and

√   conduct a face-to-face interview with you to determine if you demonstrate successful compliance with the SAP's original evaluation recommendations.

If you have demonstrated successful compliance, the SAP must send a written report to the DER.

The SAP may determine that you have successfully demonstrated compliance even though you have not completed the treatment and/or education prescribed by the SAP or if you need additional assistance.

If you haven't demonstrated successful compliance, the SAP must send a written report to the DER. Your employer may not return you to safety-sensitive functions. Also, your employer may take action based on your company policy.

§40.303 What happens if the SAP believes the employee needs additional treatment, aftercare, or support group services even after the employee returns to safety-sensitive duties?

If the SAP believes that ongoing services are needed to help you stay sober or stay away from drug use after you resume safety-sensitive functions, the SAP must provide recommendations for these services in the follow-up evaluation report.

Your employer may, as part of a return-to-duty agreement with you, require you to participate in the recommended services.

Your employer may monitor and document your participation and make use of SAP and employee assistance program services in assisting and monitoring your compliance with the SAP's recommendations.

You are required to comply with the SAP's recommendations. If you don't comply, you may be subject to disciplinary action by your employer.

§40.305 How does the return-to-duty process conclude?

In order to return to the performance of safety-sensitive functions, you must:

√ successfully comply with the education and/or treatment prescribed by the SAP; and

√ take a return-to-duty test with a negative drug test result and/or alcohol test with an alcohol concentration of less than 0.02.

Your employer is not required to return you to safety-sensitive functions because you met the return-to-duty requirements. This will be based on company policy and other legal requirements.

The SAP or MRO may not make a "fitness for duty" determination as part of this re-evaluation. It is your employer who must decide whether to put you back to work in a safety-sensitive position.

§40.307 What is the SAP's function in prescribing the employee's follow-up tests?

The SAP must establish a written follow-up testing plan. This plan will be established after you have successfully complied with the SAP's recommendations for education and/or treatment. A copy of the plan must be presented directly to the DER.

The SAP is the sole determiner of the number and frequency of follow-up tests and whether these test will be for drugs, alcohol, or both.

You will be subject to a minimum of six unannounced follow-up tests in the first 12 months of safety-sensitive duty following your return to safety-sensitive functions.

The SAP may require additional follow-up tests during the first 12-month period, and may require additional follow-up tests for an additional 48 months following the first 12-month period.

The SAP may not set specific dates for the follow-up tests. Your employer will set the dates.

Your employer may not impose additional testing requirements that go beyond the SAP's follow-up testing plan.

Should you change employers or not work in safety-sensitive functions, the requirements of the SAP's follow-up testing plan still apply.

Other than the six follow-up tests in the first 12 months, the SAP may modify the follow-up testing requirements he/she prescribed.

§40.309 What are the employer's responsibilities with respect to the SAP's directions for follow-up tests?

Your employer must carry out the SAP's follow-up testing requirements. Your employer may not let you continue to perform safety-sensitive functions unless follow-up testing is conducted as directed by the SAP.

Your employer must schedule the dates of follow-up testing, but must ensure that there isn't a pattern to the timing of the tests and that you are given no advance notice.

Other tests (random, post-accident) may not be substituted for a follow-up test.

A cancelled follow-up test may not be counted as a completed test. A cancelled follow-up test must be recollected.

§40.311 What are the requirements concerning SAP reports?

The SAP conducting the required evaluations must send the written reports directly to the

DER. However, the SAP may send the reports to the DER and C/TPA at the same time.

The SAP's written report, following the initial evaluation that determines what level of assistance is needed to address your drug and/or alcohol problems must be on the SAP's letterhead, signed and dated by the SAP and include information about you, your employer, the reason for your assessment, the SAP's treatment recommendation, and the SAP's determination as to whether you have demonstrated successful compliance.

The SAP's written report, following the follow-up evaluation that determines you have demonstrated successful compliance must be on the SAP's letterhead, signed and dated by the SAP and include information about you, your employer, the reason for your assessment, the SAP's treatment recommendation, and the SAP's determination as to whether you have demonstrated successful compliance.

The SAP's written report, following the follow-up evaluation that determines you haven't demonstrated successful compliance must be on the SAP's letterhead, signed and dated by the SAP, and include information about you, your employer, the reason for your assessment, the SAP's treatment recommendation, and the SAP's reasons for determining that you have not demonstrated successful compliance.

The SAP must also provide these written reports directly to you if you don't have a current employer and to any other DOT regulated employer you may perform safety-sensitive functions for as a new hire.

The SAP and your employer must keep these reports for 5 years.

Subpart P — Confidentiality and Release of Information

§40.321 What is the general confidentiality rule for drug and alcohol test information?

Your employer and any other service agent involved in the drug and alcohol testing process is prohibited from releasing your test results or any other medical information to third parties without your specific written consent.

"Blanket releases," in which you agree to the release of a category of information (for example, all test results) or release information to a category of parties (for example, other employers) are prohibited.

§40.323 May program participants release drug or alcohol test information in connection with legal proceedings?

Your employer may release your drug and alcohol test information without your consent in certain legal proceedings including lawsuits, grievances, and civil and criminal proceedings.

This information may only be released to the decisionmaker in the proceeding with a binding stipulation that the information will only be made available to parties to the proceeding.

Your employer or the employer's service agent must immediately notify you in writing of any information released under these circumstances.

§40.327 When must the MRO report medical information gathered in the verification process?

The medical review officer (MRO) may report drug test results and medical information learned as part of the verification process to third parties if the MRO determines that:

√ the information would likely result in you being deemed medically unqualified; or

√ the information indicated that your continued performance of safety-sensitive functions could pose a safety risk.

Third parties to whom the MRO may release this information include:

√ your employer;

√ a physician or other health care provider responsible for determining your medical qualification;

√ a substance abuse professional (SAP) evaluating you as part of the return-to-duty process;

√ a DOT agency; or

√ the National Transportation Safety Board for accident investigation purposes.

§40.329 What information must laboratories, MROs, and other service agents release to employees?

When an MRO or service agent receives a written request from you for copies of any records pertaining to your use of alcohol and/or drugs, including records of your mandated tests, he/she must provide them within 10 business days.

When a laboratory receives a written request from you (made through the MRO) for copies of records relating to your drug test, it must provide them within 10 business days.

The MRO, service agent, or laboratory may only charge you the cost of preparation and reproduction of these records.

§40.331 To what additional parties must employers and service agents release information?

Your employer must release information when you give written permission for the release of information about your drug and alcohol tests to an identified person.

Your employer and service agents must, upon request of DOT agency representatives, provide access to the company's facilities and provide all written, printed, and computer-based drug and alcohol program records, reports, and files.

All drug and alcohol program records must be easily accessible, legible, and provided in an organized manner. If electronic records do not meet these standards, they must be converted to printed documents that meet the standards.

Your employer and service agents are also required to release drug and alcohol program information as part of an accident investigation or if the records are requested by a regulatory safety agency.

§40.333 What records must employers keep?

Your employer must keep the following records for 5 years:

√ alcohol test results with a concentration of 0.02 or greater;

√ verified positive drug test results;

√ documentation of refusals to take required alcohol and/or drug tests;

√ SAP reports; and

√ all follow-up tests and schedules for follow-up tests.

Drug and alcohol test result records obtained from previous employers must be kept for 3 years.

Records of the inspection, maintenance, and calibration of EBTs must be kept for 2 years.

Records of negative and cancelled drug tests and alcohol test results with a concentration of less than 0.02 must be kept for 1 year.

All of the records must be kept in a location with controlled access. The records may be kept at a service agent's facility, but your employer must be able to produce them when requested by an inspector.

If the records are stored electronically, your employer must ensure that the records are easily accessible, legible, and formatted. They must be stored in an organized manner.

If the electronic records do not meet these criteria, your employer must be able to convert them to printed documents. The documents must be legible and able to be printed quickly at the request of the DOT.

Subpart Q — Roles and Responsibilities of Service Agents

§40.341 Must service agents comply with DOT drug and alcohol testing requirements?

The service agent's services must meet the Department of Transportation (DOT) regulatory requirements. A service agent that doesn't comply may be subject to action under the Public Interest Exclusion (PIE) procedures. (*see Part 40, Subpart R*)

§40.345 In what circumstances may a C/TPA act as an intermediary in the transmission of drug and alcohol testing information to employers?

A consortium/third party administrator (C/TPA) or other service agent may act as an intermediary under certain circumstances. (*see Part 40, Appendix F*) The C/TPA or service agent must ensure that the transmission of information to your employer meets all confidentiality and timing requirements.

§40.347 What functions may C/TPAs perform with respect to administering testing?

A C/TPA may operate random testing programs and assist with other types of testing (pre-employment, post-accident, etc.).

A C/TPA may combine employees from more than one employer in a random pool.

A C/TPA may assist your employer in ensuring that follow-up testing is conducted according to a plan established by a substance abuse professional (SAP).

§40.349 What records may a service agent receive and maintain?

A service agent may receive all DOT drug and alcohol testing records. This includes your positive, negative, and refusal to test results. A service agent doesn't need your consent to receive and keep these records.

The service agent may keep all information needed for operating a drug/alcohol program for your employer.

The service agent must be able to make available to your employer, within 2 business days, any information your employer is asked to produce by a DOT agent.

At the request of your employer, the service agent must immediately transfer all records to your employer or any other service agent your employer chooses. Your permission is not needed for the transfer.

If the service agent goes out of business, or is bought out or merged with another company, your employer must be notified. The service agent must also offer to transfer the records to your employer or another service agent. Your permission is not needed for the transfer.

§40.351 What confidentiality requirements apply to service agents?

When a service agent receives or keeps confidential information about you, he/she must follow the same confidentiality and record retention requirements as your employer.

The service agent may not provide your test results or other confidential information without your specific, written permission. A blanket consent form authorizing the release of your testing information is not permitted.

The service agent must have in place measures to ensure that your records are not available to unauthorized persons.

§40.355 What limitations apply to the activities of service agents?

A service agent may not:

√ require you to sign a consent, release, or waiver of liability connected with the DOT drug or alcohol testing process (no one may do so on behalf of the service agent);

√ act as a middle-man in the sending of drug test results from the lab to the medical review officer (MRO);

√ send drug test results directly from the lab to your employer (they must be processed by the MRO first);

√ act as a middle-man in the sending of alcohol test results of 0.02 or higher from the screening test technician (STT) or breath alcohol technician (BAT) to the designated employer representative (DER);

√ act as a middle-man in the sending of SAP reports to your employer;

√ make decisions to test you based on reasonable suspicion, post-accident, return-to-duty, and follow-up determination criteria;

√ make the decision that you have refused a drug or alcohol test;

√ act as a DER;

√ impose other conditions or requirements on your employer that DOT regulations do not allow; and

√ intentionally delay the sending of drug or alcohol testing-related documents for any reason.

PART 383 — COMMERCIAL DRIVER'S LICENSE STANDARDS; REQUIREMENTS AND PENALTIES

The **exact wording** of the regulations in this section appears in Part 383 of the Federal Motor Carrier Safety Regulations.

Editor's Note: You must comply with all of the Part 383 regulations if you drive a vehicle that:

√ has a gross combination weight rating (GCWR) of 26,001 pounds or more including a towed unit with a gross vehicle weight rating (GVWR) more than 10,000 pounds;

√ has a GVWR of 26,001 pounds or more;

√ is designed to transport 16 or more people, including the driver; or

√ is of any size and transports a placardable amount of hazardous materials or any quantity of a material listed as a select agent or toxin (see 42CFR Part 73).

Exceptions — There are certain exceptions for military drivers. A state may also allow certain exceptions for farmers, firefighters, emergency response vehicle drivers, drivers removing snow and ice, and drivers in the fireworks industry.

Subpart A — General

§383.1 Purpose and scope.

The purpose of Part 383 is to reduce or prevent truck and bus accidents, deaths, and injuries by requiring drivers to have a single commercial motor vehicle driver's license and by disqualifying drivers who operate commercial motor vehicles in an unsafe manner.

This part:

√ prohibits you from having more than one commercial motor vehicle driver's license;

√ requires you to notify your current employer and the state where you live of certain convictions;

√ requires that you provide previous employment information when applying for a job as a driver of a commercial motor vehicle;

√ prohibits your employer from allowing you to drive a commercial motor vehicle if you have a suspended license;

√ establishes periods of disqualification and penalties if you are convicted of certain criminal and other offenses and serious traffic violations, or subject to any suspensions, revocations, or cancellations of certain driving privileges;

√ establishes testing and licensing requirements to drive a commercial motor vehicle;

√ requires states to give knowledge and skills tests which meet the federal standard if you are a qualified applicant for a commercial driver's license;

√ sets guidelines for commercial motor vehicle groups and endorsements;

√ sets guidelines for the knowledge and skills test requirements for the motor vehicle groups and endorsements;

§383.3

√ sets federal standards for procedures, methods, and minimum passing scores for states and others to use in testing and licensing commercial motor vehicle drivers; and

√ establishes requirements for the state issued commercial license documentation.

§383.3 Applicability.

Part 383 applies to all people who operate a commercial motor vehicle (CMV) in interstate, foreign, or intrastate commerce, all employers of such people, and all states.

Subpart B — Single License Requirement

§383.21 Number of drivers' licenses.

If you operate a commercial motor vehicle you may not have more than one driver's license.

§383.23 Commercial driver's license.

You may not operate a commercial motor vehicle unless you have taken and passed written and driving tests which meet the federal standards contained in Subparts F, G, and H of Part 383 for the commercial motor vehicle that you drive or expect to drive.

You may not drive a commercial motor vehicle unless you have a commercial driver's license (CDL) which meets the standards contained in Subpart J of Part 383, issued by the state where you live.

A state learner's permit, issued for a limited time period, according to state requirements, is considered a valid CDL for purposes of behind-the-wheel training on public roads or highways, if the following minimum conditions are met:

√   the learner's permit holder must be with the holder of a valid CDL at all times;

√   the holder of the learner's permit either holds a valid automobile driver's license, or has passed such vision, sign/symbol, and knowledge tests as the state issuing the learner's permit ordinarily administers to applicants for automobile drivers' licenses; and

√   the learner's permit holder does not operate a commercial motor vehicle transporting a placardable amount of hazardous materials or any quantity of a material listed as a select agent or toxin *(see 42CFR Part 73)*.

Subpart C — Notification Requirements and Employer Responsibilities

§383.31 Notification of convictions for driver violations.

You must notify your employer and the state that issued your driver's license of any motor vehicle violation within 30 days after you have been convicted.

Notification to the state and your employer must be in writing and contain the following information:

√   your full name;

√   your driver's license number;

√   date of conviction;

√   the specific offense or violation and any suspension, revocation, or cancellation of driving privileges as a result of the conviction;

√   indication of whether the violation was in a commercial motor vehicle;

√   location of the offense; and

√   your signature.

§383.33 Notification of driver's license suspensions.

If you have your driver's license suspended, revoked, or cancelled, disqualifying you from operating a commercial motor vehicle, you must notify your employer before the end of the business day, the day after you received notice.

§383.35 Notification of previous employment.

If you are applying for a job as a driver of a commercial motor vehicle, you must give the following job history information for the past 10 years:

√   a list of the names and addresses of the previous employer(s) for which you drove a commercial motor vehicle;

√   the dates you worked for the employer(s); and

√   the reason for leaving the employer(s).

You must also certify that all of the information you listed is true and complete.

Your prospective employer may ask for additional application information and must let you know that any information you provide regarding your past jobs and employers may be used to investigate your past work history.

§383.37 Employer responsibilities.

Your employer may not knowingly allow, require, permit, or authorize you to drive a commercial motor vehicle:

√ during any period in which you have a commercial motor vehicle driver's license suspended, revoked, or canceled by a state, have lost the right to operate a commercial motor vehicle in a state, or have been disqualified from operating a commercial motor vehicle;

√ during any period in which you have more than one commercial motor vehicle driver's license;

√ during any period in which you, the commercial motor vehicle you are driving, or your employer is subject to an out-of-service order; or

√ in violation of a federal, state, or local law or regulation pertaining to railroad-highway grade crossings.

Subpart D — Driver Disqualification and Penalties

Editor's Note: Disqualification means any of the following three actions:

1. The suspension, revocation, or cancellation of your CDL by the state or jurisdiction of issuance.

2. Any withdrawal of your privileges to drive a commercial motor vehicle (CMV) by a state or other jurisdiction as the result of a violation of state or local law relating to motor vehicle traffic control (other than parking, vehicle weight, or vehicle defect violations).

3. A determination by the Federal Motor Carrier Safety Administration (FMCSA) that you are not qualified to operate a CMV under Part 391.

§383.51 Disqualification of drivers.

If you are disqualified, you may not drive a CMV and your employer may not allow, require, permit, or authorize you to drive a CMV.

Major offenses. You are disqualified from driving if you are convicted (including forfeiture of bond or collateral) of any of the following major offenses while driving a CMV or non-CMV:

√ being under the influence of alcohol as prescribed by state law;

√ being under the influence of a controlled substance;

√ refusing to take an alcohol test as requested by a state or jurisdiction under its implied consent laws or regulations (*see §383.72*);

√ leaving the scene of an accident;

√ using a vehicle to commit a felony; or

√ using a vehicle in the commission of a felony involving the manufacturing, distributing, or dispensing of a controlled substance.

You are disqualified from driving if you are convicted (including forfeiture of bond or collateral) of any of the following major or offenses while driving a CMV:

√ having an alcohol concentration of 0.04 or greater;

√ driving a CMV when, as a result of prior violations committed operating a CMV, your commercial driver's license (CDL) is revoked, suspended, or canceled, or you are disqualified from operating a CMV or;

√ causing a fatality through the negligent operation of a CMV.

If you are convicted of an offense described above (with the exception of using a vehicle to commit a felony involving manufacturing, distributing, or dispensing a drug), you are disqualified for a period of 1 year, provided the vehicle you are driving is not transporting a placardable amount of hazardous materials.

If you are convicted of an offense described above (with the exception of using a vehicle to commit a felony involving manufacturing, distributing, or dispensing a drug), and are transporting hazardous materials the disqualification period is 3 years.

If you are convicted a second time of an offense described above (with the exception of using a vehicle to commit a felony involving manufacturing, distributing, or dispensing a drug), you are disqualified for life.

If you are convicted of using a vehicle to commit a felony involving manufacturing, distributing, or dispensing a drug, you are disqualified for life and are not eligible for reinstatement.

If you have been disqualified for life, and have both voluntarily enrolled in and successfully completed, an appropriate rehabilitation program approved by your state, you may apply for reinstatement. You are not eligible for reinstatement from the state unless you have first served a minimum disqualification period of 10 years and have fully met the licensing state's standards for reinstatement.

Should you, as a reinstated driver, be convicted of another disqualifying offense, you will be permanently disqualified for life, and ineligible to again apply for a reduction of the lifetime disqualification.

Serious traffic violations. You are disqualified from driving a CMV if you are convicted (including forfeiture of bond or collateral) of any of the following serious offenses while driving a CMV or non-CMV *(see **Editor's Note** on pg. 199)*:

√ excessive speeding, 15 mph or more above the posted speed limit;

√ reckless driving;

√ improper or erratic traffic lane changes;

√ following the vehicle ahead too closely;

√ violating state or local law relating to motor vehicle traffic control (other than a parking violation) arising in connection with a fatal accident;

√ driving a CMV without obtaining a CDL (not applicable to non-CMV operations);

√ driving a CMV without a CDL in your possession (not applicable to non-CMV operations); or

√ driving a CMV without proper class of CDL and/or endorsements for the specific vehicle group being operated or for the passengers or type of cargo being transported (not applicable to non-CMV operations).

If you are convicted of two serious traffic violations in separate incidents during any 3-year period, you are disqualified for a period of 60 days.

If you are convicted of three serious traffic violations in separate incidents during any 3-year period, you are disqualified for a period of 120 days.

Editor's Note: A driver convicted of two or more serious traffic violations while operating a non-CMV is disqualified only if the conviction results in the revocation, cancellation, or suspension of the driver's license or driving privileges.

Editor's Note: In Part 383 an out-of-service order means an authorized enforcement officer of a federal, state, Canadian, Mexican, or local jurisdiction has declared that you, your commercial motor vehicle, or your carrier's operation is out of service according to §§386.72, 392.5, 395.13, 396.9, or compatible laws, or the North American Uniform Out-of-Service Criteria.

Out-of-service violation. If you are convicted of violating an out-of-service order you are subject to a disqualification period.

The regulations contain the following penalty structure for drivers:

√ first conviction — disqualification for 180 days to 1 year;

√ second conviction in a separate incident during a 10 year period — disqualification for 2 to 5 years;

√ third or subsequent conviction in a separate incident during a 10 year period — disqualification for 3 to 5 years.

The penalties are more severe for bus drivers and drivers of vehicles carrying hazardous materials. The penalty for the first conviction is 180 days to 2 years. A second or third conviction in a separate incident during a 10 year period will result in a 3 to 5 year disqualification.

Editor's Note: Certain types of vehicles are required to stop at all railroad crossings. See §392.10 for specific details.

Railroad-highway grade crossing violation. You are disqualified from driving if you are convicted of any one of the following six offenses at a railroad-highway grade crossing while driving a CMV:

√ failing to slow down (if you are *not* required to stop at all times) and check that the tracks are clear of an approaching train;

√ failing to stop (if you are *not* required to stop at all times) before reaching the crossing if the tracks are not clear;

√ failing to stop (if you are required to stop at all times) before driving onto the crossing;

√ failing to have sufficient space to drive completely through the crossing without stopping;

√ failing to obey a traffic control device or the directions of an enforcement officer at the crossing; or

√ failing to negotiate a crossing because of insufficient undercarriage clearance.

If you are convicted of a railroad-highway grade crossing violation you are subject to a disqualification period.

The regulations contain the following penalty structure for drivers:

√ first conviction — disqualification for at least 60 days;

√ second conviction in a separate incident during a 3 year period — disqualification for at least 120 days;

√ third or subsequent conviction in a separate incident during a 3 year period — disqualification for at least 1 year.

§383.52 Disqualification of drivers determined to constitute an imminent hazard.

Editor's Note: In Part 383 an imminent hazard means the existence of a condition that presents a substantial likelihood of death, serious illness, or severe personal injury, or a substantial endangerment to health, property, or the environment may occur before the reasonably foreseeable completion date of a formal proceeding begun to lessen the risk of that death, illness, injury, or endangerment.

The Federal Motor Carrier Safety Administration's (FMCSA) Assistant Administrator or his/her designee must disqualify you from operating a commercial motor vehicle (CMV) if your driving is determined to constitute an imminent hazard.

The period of disqualification may not exceed 30 days, unless the FMCSA follows certain provisions as explained below.

If you are issued a disqualification for 30 days or less, the FMCSA's Assistant Administrator or his/her designee may provide you the opportunity for a hearing.

If you are issued a disqualification for more than 30 days, the FMCSA's Assistant Administrator or his/her designee must provide you notice of this proposed disqualification and the opportunity for a hearing.

The disqualification period may not exceed 1 year and you may file an appeal of the disqualification.

Any disqualification must be forwarded by the FMCSA to the jurisdiction where you are licensed and must become a part of your driving record.

§383.53 Penalties.

Fines for violating an out-of-service order range from $2,500 to $5,000 (in addition to disqualification) for drivers and $2,750 to $25,000 for employers.

The fine for an employer who is convicted of knowingly allowing, permitting, or authorizing a driver to violate a railroad-highway grade crossing regulation is up to $10,000.

Subpart E — Testing and Licensing Procedures

§383.71 Driver application procedures.

Before getting a commercial driver's license, you must meet the following requirements:

√ if you plan to drive in interstate or foreign commerce you must certify that you meet the requirements listed in Part 391;

√ if you operate entirely intrastate and are not subject to the requirements listed in Part 391, you must follow state driver qualification requirements and must certify that you are not subject to Part 391;

√ pass a knowledge test for the type of vehicle(s) you expect to drive;

√ pass a driving or skills test taken in a motor vehicle like the type you expect to drive or present evidence that you passed a driving test given by an authorized third party;

√ certify that the motor vehicle in which you take the driving skills test is like the type of vehicle you will be driving;

√ give the state you will receive your commercial driver's license (CDL) from the information required to be included on the CDL (includes name, address, birthdate, etc.);

√ certify that you are not subject to any disqualification under §383.51, or any license suspension, revocation, or cancellation under state law;

√ certify that you do not have a driver's license from more than one state or jurisdiction;

√ you must give your non-CDL driver's license to the state; and

√ provide the names of all states where you have previously been licensed to drive any type of motor vehicle during the previous 10 years.

If you are applying for a hazardous materials endorsement, compliance with the Transportation Security Administration (TSA) requirements in 49CFR Part 1572 is required. You must also provide proof of citizenship or immigration status as specified in the following table:

Acceptable Proof of Citizenship or Immigration	
Status	**Proof of Status**
U.S. Citizen	U.S. passport
	Birth certificate that bears an official seal and was issued by a state, county, municipal authority, or outlying possession of the United States
	Certification of birth abroad issued by U.S. Department of State
	Certificate of naturalization
	Certificate of U.S. citizenship
Lawful Permanent Resident	Permanent resident card, alien registration receipt card
	Temporary I-551 stamp in foreign passport
	Temporary I-551 stamp on Form I-94, arrival/departure record, with photograph of the bearer
	Reentry permit

If you are a lawful permanent resident of the United States requesting a hazardous materials endorsement, you must also provide your Bureau of Citizenship and Immigration Services (BCIS) Alien registration number.

If you apply to transfer a CDL from the state where you live to a new home in a different state, you must apply for a CDL from your new home state within 30 days after establishing your new residency. You must:

√ provide to your new home state the certifications for an initial license listed above;

√ give your new home state updated information as listed in Part 383 Subpart J;

√ follow the TSA and proof of citizenship or immigration status requirements for such endorsement *(see §383.71(a)(9))* and the state requirements as listed in §383.73(b)(4) (if you wish to keep a hazardous materials endorsement);

√ give your CDL from your old state of residency to your new home state; and

√ provide the names of all states where you have previously been licensed to drive any type of motor vehicle during the previous 10 years.

When applying for renewal of a CDL, you must:

√   provide certification that you meet the requirements listed in Part 391 (if you drive interstate);

√   certify that you are not subject to the requirements listed in Part 391 (if you operate entirely intrastate and are not subject to Part 391);

√   provide updated information as listed in Part 383 Subpart J;

√   comply with the TSA and proof of citizenship or immigration status requirements *(see §383.71(a)(9))*;

√   pass a hazardous materials endorsement test *(see §383.121)* if you wish to keep a hazardous materials endorsement; and

√   provide the names of all states where you have previously been licensed to drive any type of motor vehicle during the previous 10 years.

If you apply to drive a commercial motor vehicle in a different group or endorsement than what you are already licensed to drive, you must give the same information and pass the same tests as someone who is applying for his/her first commercial driver's license.

To obtain a hazardous materials endorsement, you must comply with the TSA requirements and be able to provide proof of citizenship or immigration status.

Subpart F — Vehicle Groups and Endorsements

§383.91 Commercial motor vehicle groups.

If you are applying for a commercial driver's license, you must pass knowledge and skills tests for the type of commercial motor vehicle(s) you want to drive. The groups are:

√ **Combination Vehicle (Group A)** — Any combination of vehicles with a gross combination weight rating (GCWR) of 26,001 pounds or more provided the gross vehicle weight rating (GVWR) of the vehicle(s) being towed is more than 10,000 pounds.

√ **Heavy Straight Vehicle (Group B)** — Any single vehicle with a GVWR of 26,001 pounds or more or a vehicle with a

GVWR of 26,001 pounds towing a vehicle with a GVWR of 10,000 pounds or less.

√ **Small Vehicle (Group C)** — Any single vehicle or combination of vehicles that do not fall into the above groups but are used to transport 16 or more passengers including the driver, or are used to transport a placardable amount of hazardous materials.

The following chart shows the types of vehicles included in each vehicle group.

Figure 1

VEHICLE GROUPS AS ESTABLISHED BY FHWA (SECTION 383.91)

[Note: Certain types of vehicles, such as passenger and doubles/triples, will require an endorsement. Please consult text for particulars.]

Group: *Description:

A   Any combination of vehicles with a GCWR of 26,001 or more pounds provided the GVWR of the vehicle(s) being towed is in excess of 10,000 pounds. (Holders of a Group A license may, with any appropriate endorsements, operate all vehicles within Groups B and C.)

Examples include but are not limited to:

B   Any single vehicle with a GVWR of 26,001 or more pounds, or any such vehicle towing a vehicle not in excess of 10,000 pounds GVWR (Holders of a Group B license may, with any appropriate endorsements, operate all vehicles within Group C.)

Examples include but are not limited to:

C   Any single vehicle, or combination of vehicles, that does not meet the definition of Group A or Group B as contained herein, but that either is designed to transport 16 or more passengers including the driver, or is placarded for hazardous materials.

Examples include but are not limited to:

*The representative vehicle for the skills test must meet the written description for that group. The silhouettes typify, but do not fully cover, the types of vehicles falling within each group.

§383.93 Endorsements.

If you plan on driving a vehicle that requires an endorsement on your license, you must take and pass a specialized test for each endorsement.

You must get an endorsement on your license to operate:

√ double/triple trailers;

√ passenger vehicles;

√ tank vehicles;

√ vehicles used to transport hazardous materials; or

√ school buses.

You are required to take a written test to get an endorsement for doubles/triples, tankers, and vehicles carrying a placardable amount of hazardous materials. You are required to take both a written and road test to get a passenger or school bus endorsement.

§383.95 Air brake restrictions.

If you fail the air brake knowledge test or take your behind-the-wheel test in a vehicle that doesn't have air brakes, your license will have a restriction that says you may not drive a vehicle with air brakes.

Subpart G — Required Knowledge and Skills

§383.110 General requirement.

To drive a commercial motor vehicle you must have a certain amount of skill as well as knowledge on how to drive the vehicle safely.

§383.111 Required knowledge.

You must have knowledge of the driver-related portions of the Federal Motor Carrier Safety Regulations. This includes knowledge of:

√ motor vehicle inspection, repair, and maintenance;

√ procedures for safe vehicle operations;

√ the effects of poor health, vision, hearing, fatigue;

√ the types of vehicles and cargos that fall under the regulations; and

√ the effects of alcohol and drug use.

Safety Systems — You must know how to use all of the vehicle's safety systems including horn, lights, mirrors, fire extinguisher, etc. You must also know what to do in an emergency situation.

Vehicle Control — You are required to know how to control your vehicle. The skills you need to know include (but are not limited to) shifting, backing, speed and space management, night driving, emergency maneuvers, and skid control and recovery.

Cargo — You must know how to properly handle cargo.

Vehicle Inspections — You must understand the importance of performing proper vehicle inspections, what to look for when performing an inspection, and how to report your findings.

Hazardous Materials — You must know what materials need a hazardous materials endorsement in order to be transported, the classes of hazardous materials, and labeling and placarding requirements.

Air Brakes — You must understand air brakes including the dangers of a contaminated air supply, cut or disconnected air lines between the power unit and trailer, and low air pressure readings. You must also know how to do pre- and post-trip inspections on air brake systems.

Combination Vehicles — You must know how to properly couple and uncouple a tractor and trailer. You must also know how to properly conduct a pre- and post-trip inspection on a combination vehicle.

§383.113 Required skills.

In order to get a commercial driver's license (CDL), you must be able to show that you can safely drive a commercial motor vehicle. The skills you need to demonstrate include starting and stopping your vehicle, and moving your vehicle forward and backward safely.

Safe Driving — You must be able to use proper visual search methods, properly use turn signals, control your speed for weather and traffic conditions, and properly position your vehicle when changing lanes or turning.

Air Brakes — You must be able to conduct a proper pre-trip inspection and show that you can safely drive a vehicle equipped with air brakes.

All skills tests must be done over the road or both on and off the road.

§383.115 Requirements for double/triple trailers endorsement.

In order to get a double/triple trailers endorsement you must know:

√ the procedures for assembly and hookup of the units;

√ the proper placement of the heaviest trailer;

√ the handling and stability basics of doubles and triples; and

√ the potential traffic problems of doubles and triples.

§383.117 Requirements for passenger endorsement.

In order to get a passenger endorsement you must know the proper procedures for:

√ loading and unloading passengers;

√ the use of emergency exits (including push-out windows);

√ responding to emergency situations (fires, unruly passengers, etc.);

√ dealing with railroad crossings and draw-bridges; and

√ braking.

You must also pass a skills test in the type of passenger vehicle you will be operating.

§383.119 Requirements for tank vehicle endorsement.

In order to get a tank vehicle endorsement you must know the following:

√ the causes, prevention, and effects of cargo surge on motor vehicle handling;

√ proper braking for a full, partially full, or empty vehicle;

√ the differences in handling a baffled or non-baffled vehicle;

√ the differences in tank vehicle type and construction;

√ the differences in cargo surge for liquids of varying densities;

√ the effects of road grade and curve;

√ the proper use of emergency systems; and

√ for drivers of DOT specification tank vehicles, retest and marking requirements.

§383.121 Requirements for hazardous materials endorsement.

In order to get a hazardous materials endorsement you must have knowledge of the hazardous materials regulations, hazardous materials handling, the operation of emergency equipment, and emergency response procedures.

The information you must understand is found in 49 CFR Parts 171, 172, 173, 177, 178, and 397.

§383.123 Requirements for a school bus endorsement.

In order to get a school bus endorsement, you must satisfy the following three requirements:

1. You must pass the knowledge and skills test for obtaining a passenger vehicle endorsement.

2. You must have knowledge covering at least the following three topics:

    √ Loading and unloading children, including the safe operation of stop signal devices, external mirror systems, flashing lights, and other warning and passenger safety devices required for school buses by state or federal law or regulation.

√ Emergency exits and procedures for safely evacuating passengers in an emergency.

√ State and federal laws and regulations related to safely crossing highway rail grade crossings.

3. You must take a driving skills test in a school bus of the same vehicle group as you will be driving. *(see §383.91(a))*

Knowledge and skills tests administered before September 30, 2002, and approved by FMCSA as meeting certain requirements, meet the requirements of 2. and 3. listed above.

Waiver — At the discretion of a state, the driving skills test may be waived if you are currently licensed, have experience driving a school bus, have a good driving record, and can certify (the state must also verify) that during the 2 year period immediately before applying for the school bus endorsement, you:

√ held a valid commercial driver's license (CDL) with a passenger vehicle endorsement to operate a school bus within the group of vehicles you will be driving;

√ have not had your driver's license or CDL suspended, revoked, or canceled, or have been disqualified from operating a commercial motor vehicle (CMV);

√ have not been convicted of a disqualifying offense; *(see §383.51))*

√ have not had more than one conviction of any serious traffic violation while operating any type of motor vehicle;

√ have not had any conviction for a violation of state or local law relating to motor vehicle traffic control (other than a parking violation) in connection with any traffic accident;

√ have not been convicted of any motor vehicle traffic violation that resulted in an accident; and

√ have been regularly employed as a school bus driver, have operated a school bus within the group of vehicles you will drive, and can provide evidence of such employment.

Note: After September 30, 2006, this waiver no longer applies.

Appendix to Subpart G — Required Knowledge and Skills — Sample Guidelines

Editor's Note: See the Federal Motor Carrier Safety Regulations for details.

Subpart H — Tests

§383.131 Test procedures.

Your state must make a manual available that explains the procedures, requirements, and skills needed to get a commercial driver's license (CDL).

All state examiners must be qualified to give tests based on training and/or experience. The state must provide examiners with a manual covering testing details and state requirements.

§383.133 Testing methods.

Each state is allowed to devise its own tests as long as the tests meet or exceed federal requirements.

§383.135 Minimum passing scores.

A passing grade is a score of at least 80 percent on a knowledge test. On a skills test you must show that you can perform all of the skills listed in §383.113.

You will automatically fail the test if you do not obey traffic laws or cause an accident.

If you score below 80 percent on the air brake portion of the written test or if you take the skills test in a vehicle without air brakes, an air brake restriction will be listed on your license.

Subpart I — Requirement for Transportation Security Administration Approval of Hazardous Materials Endorsement Issuances

§383.141 General.

A state may not issue, renew, upgrade, or transfer a hazardous materials endorsement on your CDL until the Transportation Security Administration (TSA) has determinded that you do not pose a security risk.

If TSA determines you pose a security risk, the state will not issue, renew, upgrade, or transfer a hazardous materials endorsement.

At least 60 days before your CDL or hazardous materials endorsement expires, you will be notified by the state that issues your license that you must pass a TSA security screening as part of the renewal process.

Once you have received notice, you should file a renewal application as soon as possible, but no later than 30 days before the endorsement expires.

If you do not pass the TSA security screening process you will not be issued a hazardous materials endorsement.

The state is required to renew your hazardous materials endorsement at least every 5 years. This means you will be subject to a TSA security screening at least every 5 years.

PART 391 — QUALIFICATIONS OF DRIVERS

The **exact wording** of the regulations in this section appears in Part 391 of the Federal Motor Carrier Safety Regulations.

Editor's Note: You must comply with all of the Part 391 regulations if you drive a vehicle that:

√ has a gross vehicle weight rating (GVWR), gross combination weight rating (GCWR), gross vehicle weight (GVW), or gross combination weight (GCW) of 10,001 pounds or more (whichever is greater);

√ is designed or used to transport more than 15 passengers (including the driver);

√ is designed or used to transport between 9 and 15 passengers (including the driver) for direct compensation, provided the vehicle is being operated beyond a 75 air-mile radius (86.3 statute miles) of your normal work reporting location; or

√ transports a placardable amount of hazardous materials.

Subpart A — General

§391.1 Scope of the rules in this part; additional qualifications; duties of carrier-drivers.

The rules in Part 391 set minimum qualification requirements that you and your employer must follow.

If you are self-employed you must follow the Part 391 requirements for both drivers and employers.

§391.2 General exemptions.

There are certain exemptions from Part 391 for some farm vehicle drivers, custom-harvesters, and beekeepers.

Subpart B — Qualification and Disqualification of Drivers

§391.11 Qualifications of drivers.

You must be qualified in order to drive a commercial motor vehicle. You are qualified if you:

√ are at least 21 years old;

√ can read, write, and speak English well enough to do your job;

√   can drive your truck safely;

√   can pass a DOT physical exam;

√   have only one current commercial driver's license;

√   have given your employer a list of any violations you have been convicted of in the past 12 months (§391.27);

√   are not disqualified to drive a commercial motor vehicle (§391.15); and

√   passed a truck driver's road test (§391.31) or have an operator's license or certificate of road test from another employer that your employer accepts as the equivalent to a road test (§391.33).

§391.13 Responsibilities of drivers.

Your employer may not permit you to drive a commercial motor vehicle unless you:

√   can determine whether the cargo you transport (including baggage in a passenger carrying vehicle) is properly loaded, distributed, and secured; and

√   are familiar with methods and procedures for securing cargo in or on the commercial motor vehicle you drive.

§391.15 Disqualification of drivers.

You are disqualified from driving a commercial motor vehicle if you are convicted of any of the following offenses while driving a commercial motor vehicle:

√ driving with an alcohol concentration of 0.04 percent or more, driving under the influence of alcohol as prescribed by state law, or refusing to undergo testing;

√ driving under the influence of a controlled substance;

√ committing a felony involving a commercial motor vehicle;

√ leaving the scene of an accident while driving a commercial motor vehicle; or

√ transporting, possessing, or unlawfully using drugs.

The disqualification period for a first conviction (with the exception of transporting, possessing, or unlawfully using drugs) is 1 year. The disqualification period for a first conviction for transporting or possessing drugs is 6 months.

If you had been convicted in the past 3 years of a disqualifying offense, another conviction will disqualify you from driving for 3 years.

If you or your vehicle is placed out-of-service by an enforcement officer, you may not continue driving until the problem that put you out-of-service is corrected.

If you are convicted of violating an out-of-service order, you will be subject to a fine and will be disqualified for the following amount of time:

√ **First violation** — disqualification for 90 days to 1 year;

√ **Second violation during a 10-year period** — disqualification for 1 to 5 years; and

√ **Three or more violations during a 10-year period** — disqualification for 3 to 5 years.

The penalties are more severe if you drive a bus or a vehicle with a placardable amount of hazardous materials. The penalty for a first violation is between 180 days and 2 years. Any more violations during the next 10 years will disqualify you for 3 to 5 years.

If you receive notice that your license, permit, or privilege to drive a commercial motor vehicle has been revoked, suspended, or withdrawn you must notify your employer before the end of the business day, the day after you receive the notice.

Subpart C — Background and Character

§391.21 Application for employment.

You may not drive a commercial motor vehicle for an employer until you have filled out a job application that includes the following information:

√ name and address of employing company;

√ your name, address, date of birth, and social security number;

√ your address(es) for the past 3 years;

√ date of application;

√ issuing state, number, and expiration date of your driver's license;

√ the type and amount of experience you have driving commercial motor vehicles;

√ list of all motor vehicle accidents you were involved in during the last 3 years (including the date and nature of each accident and any fatalities or personal injuries it caused);

√ list of all violations of motor vehicle laws and ordinances of which you were convicted and/or fined during the last 3 years;

√ a statement detailing facts and circumstances of any denial, revocation, or suspension of any license, permit, or privilege to operate a motor vehicle issued to you, or a statement that no such denial, revocation, or suspension has occurred;

√ list of the names and addresses of your employers during the last 3 years, including dates of employment;

√ the reason you left the employer;

√ (after October 29, 2004) information as to whether you were subject to the Federal Motor Carrier Safety Regulations (FMCSRs) in your job and if the job was designated a safety sensitive function, subjecting you to the Part 40 drug and alcohol testing requirements;

√ if you will operate a commercial motor vehicle that has a GVWR of 26,001 pounds or more, is designed to carry more than 15 people, or is any size used to carry a placardable amount of hazardous materials, you must also list employment for which you operated a commercial motor vehicle during the 7 years before the 3 years mentioned above (a total of 10 years); and

√ a certification statement that the information supplied is correct, your signature, and the date you filled out the application.

The company must notify you before your submission of the application that the information you provide may be used, and your previous employers will be contacted, as part of an investigation into your safety performance history.

The company must also notify you in writing of your due process rights regarding information received as a result of the investigation. *(see §391.23)*

The regulations allow the carrier to ask you for additional information as part of the application for employment.

§391.23 Investigation and inquiries.

The regulations require every motor carrier to check into the last 3 years driving records for all newly hired drivers.

Also, every motor carrier must conduct an investigation of each newly hired driver's safety performance history with Department of Transportation (DOT) regulated employers during the past 3 years.

A copy of each state agency's response regarding your driving records must be placed in your driver qualification file within 30 days of the date your employment begins. If no driving record exists from the state(s), the company must document a good faith effort to obtain this information and certify that no record exists for you in the state(s).

Replies to the investigations of your safety performance history or documentation of good faith efforts to obtain the information, must be placed in your driver investigation history file (after October 29, 2004) within 30 days of the date your employment begins.

The investigation may consist of personal interviews, telephone interviews, letters, or any other method for investigating that the motor carrier deems appropriate.

The motor carrier must make a written record of each previous employer contacted or good faith efforts to do so. The record must include the:

√ previous employer's name and address;

√ date the previous employer was contacted or the attempts made; and

√ information received from the previous employer.

Failure to contact a previous employer or failure of the previous employer to provide the required safety performance history information must be documented and this record must be maintained. *(see §391.53)*

The motor carrier should report failures of previous employers to respond to an investigation to the Federal Motor Carrier Safety Administration (FMCSA). A copy of this report should be kept in the driver investigation file to aid in documenting a good faith effort to obtain the required information.

If you haven't worked for a DOT regulated employer in the past 3 years, documentation that no investigation is possible must be placed in your driver history investigation file (after October 29, 2004) within 30 days of the date your employment begins.

At a minimum, the following information must be requested from all previous employers:

√ general driver and employment verification information;

√ accidents you have been involved in during the past 3 years;

√ whether, during the past 3 years, you violated any Part 40 or Part 382 drug and alcohol prohibitions; and

√ whether you failed to undertake or complete a substance abuse rehabilitation program as prescribed by a substance abuse professional (SAP) per §382.605 or Part 40, Subpart O during the past 3 years.

If you have successfully completed an SAP's rehabilitation referral, and remained in the employ of the referring employer, information on whether you had the following testing violations must be supplied:

√ alcohol tests with a result of 0.04 or higher;

√ verified positive drug tests; and

√ refusals to be tested (including verified adulterated or substituted results).

Your written consent to release your drug and alcohol records must be supplied to all previous employers before this information may be released to your prospective employer. If you refuse to provide this written consent, you may not operate a commercial motor vehicle for the prospective motor carrier.

After October 29, 2004, previous employers must:

√ respond to each request for the information previously listed within 30 days after the request is received;

√ take all reasonable precautions to ensure accuracy of the records;

√ provide specific contact information in the event you choose to contact the previous employer regarding correction or rebuttal of the information; and

√ keep a record of each request and the response for 1 year including the date, party to whom it was released, and a summary identifying what was provided.

The release of your safety performance history information may take any form that ensures confidentiality, including by letter, fax, or e-mail.

Your previous employer(s) and its agents and insurers must take all reasonable precautions to protect your safety performance history records from disclosure to anyone not directly involved in the process.

Note: Insurers may not be provided your alcohol and/or drug testing information.

Before a hiring decision is made, the prospective employer must notify you (via the application or other written documentation) that you have the following rights regarding the investigative information that will be provided:

√   the right to review all information provided by previous employers;

√   the right to have errors in the information corrected by the previous employer and the corrected information resent to the prospective employer; and

√   the right to have a rebuttal statement attached to alleged erroneous information if you and the previous employer cannot agree on the accuracy of the information.

You may review the information provided by the previous employer. This can be done from the time you apply for the new job up to 30 days after being employed or denied employment.

Your request to review this information must be a written request. The prospective employer then has 5 business days to provide you with the information.

If the prospective employer has yet to receive the information, the employer has 5 business days from the time the information is received to provide it to you.

You must arrange to pick-up or receive the information within 30 days of its availability. If you do not do this, the prospective employer may consider this a waiver of your request to view this information.

After reviewing the information, if you want to request a correction to the records you received, you must send your request for the correction to the previous employer that provided the records.

After October 29, 2004, the previous employer must either correct and forward the information to the prospective employer or notify you within 15 days after receiving the request for correction that it does not agree to correct the data.

Any information the previous employer corrects must be retained in your safety performance history record and provided to subsequent prospective employers when requests for information are received.

If you have a rebuttal statement regarding the records, you must send this to the previous employer with directions to include this in your safety performance history file.

After October 29, 2004, within 5 days of receiving a rebuttal from you, the previous employer must:

√ forward a copy of the rebuttal to the prospective employer; and

√ include the rebuttal in your safety performance history file.

You may report to the FMCSA any previous employer who fails to correct information as requested or refuses to include a rebuttal you submit in your safety performance history file.

The prospective employer may only use your safety performance history information as part of deciding whether to hire you.

The prospective employer must take all precautions necessary to protect these records from disclosure to any person not directly involved in the hiring process.

You may not bring an action or proceeding for defamation, invasion of privacy, or interference with a contract based on the furnishing or use of your safety performance history information against:

√ the prospective employer investigating the information;

√ the person (previous employer) who furnished the information; or

√ the agents or insurers of the prospective or previous employer (insurers are not granted limited liability on drug and/or alcohol information).

The protections listed above do not apply to anyone who knowingly furnishes false information or is not in compliance with the requirements specified for these types of investigations.

§391.25 Annual review of driving record.

At least once every 12 months your employer must request a copy of your driving record from each state in which you held a commercial motor vehicle operator's license or permit in the past 12 months.

At least once every 12 months, your employer must review your driving record, including compliance with the Federal Motor Carrier Safety Regulations and Hazardous Materials Regulations.

When reviewing your driving record, your employer should pay special attention to any accidents and incidents or violations of motor vehicle laws and regulations. This includes violations showing a disregard for public safety (speeding, reckless driving, operating a vehicle while under the influence of alcohol or drugs, etc.).

A copy of the response from each state and a note, including the name of the person who reviewed your driving record, and the date of the review, must be placed in your driver qualification file.

§391.27 Record of violations.

When you are first hired, and then once every 12 months, your employer must ask for and get from you a list of any violations of traffic laws and ordinances for which you were convicted or paid a fine in the past 12 months.

If you have no violations, you must still submit the record to your employer stating you don't have any violations.

The record must be similar to the following form.

Driver's Certification

I certify that the following is a true and complete list of traffic violations (other than parking violations) for which I have been convicted or forfeited bond or collateral during the past 12 months.

Date of conviction	Offense
————————	————————————————
————————	————————————————
————————	————————————————

Location	Type of motor vehicle operated
————————	————————————————
————————	————————————————
————————	————————————————

If no violations are listed above, I certify that I have not been convicted or forfeited bond or collateral on account of any violation required to be listed during the past 12 months.

————————————————   ————————————————
(Date of certification)   (Driver's signature)

————————————————————————————————
(Motor carrier's name)

————————————————————————————————
(Motor carrier's address)

————————————————   ————————————————
(Reviewed by: Signature)   (Title)

If you are subject to the commercial driver's license provisions in Part 383, you must notify your employer of any motor vehicle violation within 30 days. The violation(s) do not need to be included on the annual list.

The list or certificate of violations must be kept in your driver qualification file.

Subpart D — Tests

§391.31 Road test.

You may not drive a commercial motor vehicle unless you have successfully completed a road test and have been issued a certificate of driver's road test.

The road test must be conducted using the type of motor vehicle you will be driving for your employer. In order to pass the road test you must successfully complete the following tasks:

√   a pretrip inspection;

√   coupling and uncoupling a combination (if you may drive such equipment);

√   placing the vehicle in operation;

√   using the vehicle's controls and emergency equipment;

√   driving in traffic and passing other vehicles;

√   turning;

√   braking, and slowing by means other than braking; and

√ backing and parking.

Your employer is required to rate your skill in each operation on a road test form, and then sign the form. The original road test form must be kept in your driver qualification file.

If you pass the road test, your employer must fill out and sign a certificate of road test. You will be given a copy, and the original or a copy will be kept in your driver qualification file. The certificate must look like the form shown below.

CERTIFICATION OF ROAD TEST

Driver's name _____

Social Security No. _____

Operator's or Chauffeur's License No. _____

State _____

Type of power unit _____

Type of trailer(s) _____

If passenger carrier, type of bus _____

This is to certify that the above-named driver was given a road test under my supervision on _____ 20 _____ consisting of approximately _____ miles of driving.

It is my considered opinion that this driver possesses sufficient driving skill to operate safely the type of commercial motor vehicle listed above.

_____

(Signature of examiner)   (Title)

_____

(Organization and address of examiner)

§391.33 Equivalent of road test.

In place of a road test, your employer may accept:

√ a valid commercial driver's license as defined in §383.5 (not including double/triple trailer or tank vehicle endorsements) issued to you by a state that requires a road test in the type of commercial motor vehicle your employer will assign you to drive; or

√ a certificate of road test issued to you by another motor carrier in the past 3 years.

A copy of the license or certificate must be placed in your driver qualification file.

Even though you present a copy of a road test or driver's license, your employer may still require a road test as a condition of employment.

Subpart E — Physical Qualifications and Examinations

§391.41 Physical qualifications for drivers.

You may not drive a commercial motor vehicle unless you are physically qualified and carry a medical examiner's certificate stating you are physically qualified. (Note: Canadian drivers are not required to carry a medical certificate because a Canadian commercial driver's license is proof of medical fitness to drive. Cana-

dian drivers with certain medical conditions
are not allowed to drive in the U.S.)

You may not drive if you:

√ have lost a foot, leg, hand, or arm; and
have not been granted a skill performance
evaluation certificate (*see §391.49*);

√ have an impairment of a hand, finger, arm,
foot, or leg which interferes with your ability to perform normal tasks associated with
driving a commercial motor vehicle; and
have not been granted a skill performance
evaluation certificate (*see §391.49*);

√ have diabetes requiring insulin for control;

√ have heart disease, which causes you chest
pain, fainting, or shortness of breath;

√ have chest or breathing problems like
chronic asthma, emphysema, and chronic
bronchitis;

√ have high blood pressure likely to interfere
with driving;

√ have loss of movement or feeling in part of
your body;

√ have any sickness which is likely to cause loss of consciousness or any loss of ability to control a commercial motor vehicle;

√ have any mental problems likely to interfere with your ability to drive a commercial motor vehicle safely;

√ have poor vision that affects your ability to see objects that are far away (you may use glasses or contact lenses to correct your vision), objects to the side, or traffic signal colors (you may not drive if you see with only one eye);

√ have poor hearing (you must be able to hear a loud whispered voice in your better ear at not less than five feet with or without the use of a hearing aid or, pass a hearing test on a doctor's testing machine);

√ use certain drugs and dangerous substances, except that you may use such a substance or drug if the substance or drug is prescribed by a doctor who is familiar with your medical history and assigned duties and who has advised you that the prescribed substance or drug will not adversely affect your ability to safely operate a commercial motor vehicle; and

√ have a current clinical diagnosis of alcoholism.

§391.43 Medical examination; certificate of physical qualification.

Your medical examination must be done by a licensed medical examiner.

A medical examiner is defined as a person who is licensed, certified and/or registered according to state laws and regulations to perform physical examinations. The term includes, but is not limited to doctors of medicine, doctors of osteopathy, physician assistants, advanced practice nurses, and doctors of chiropractic. (*see §390.5.*)

A licensed optometrist may perform the visual portion of the exam.

The exam must be done and recorded according to the regulations.

If the medical examiner finds that you are physically qualified to drive a commercial motor vehicle, the medical examiner will fill out a medical certificate. You must keep a copy with you and a copy will be sent to your employer and put into your driver qualification file.

§391.45 Persons who must be medically examined and certified.

You must have a medical exam if:

√ you have not been medically examined and physically qualified to drive a commercial motor vehicle;

√ you have not had a medical exam in the past 24 months; or

√ you have suffered a disease or injury that affected your ability to drive a commercial motor vehicle.

§391.47 Resolution of conflicts of medical evaluation.

If you disagree with your medical evaluation you may dispute it through a detailed process with the Office of Bus and Truck Standards and Operations.

§391.49 Alternative physical qualification standards for the loss or impairment of limbs.

If you are not physically qualified to drive because of a limb impairment, you may apply to the Division Administrator, Federal Motor Carrier Safety Administration, for a Skill Performance Evaluation (SPE) certificate.

Subpart F — Files and Records

§391.51 Driver qualification files.

Your employer is required to maintain a driver qualification (DQ) file for each driver it employs. The DQ file may be combined with your personnel file.

The following documents must be included in your DQ file:

√ application for employment (§391.21);

√ response from each state agency regarding your motor vehicle record (§391.23(a)(1));

√ written record of previous employer information (§391.23);

√ road test form and certificate (§391.31(e)), or license or certificate accepted in lieu of road test (§391.33);

√ medical exam certificate — original or a copy (§391.43(f));

√ any letter granting a waiver of a physical disqualification;

√ response of each state agency to the annual review of driving record inquiry (§391.25(a));

√ a note relating to the annual review of your driving record (§391.25(c)(2)); and

√ list of violations (§391.27).

Your DQ file must be kept by your employer for the whole time you are employed by your employer plus 3 years.

The regulations also allow for the removal of outdated materials from the DQ file. This provision applies to materials which must be reviewed or updated periodically. After 3 years from the date they are filled out, the medical examiner's certificate, the response of each state agency to the annual review of driving record, the note relating to the annual review of your driving record, and the annual list of violations can be thrown away.

§391.53 Driver Investigation History File.

After October 29, 2004, each motor carrier must maintain records relating to the safety performance history of a new or prospective driver.

This file must be maintained in a secure location with controlled access.

The motor carrier must ensure that access to this data is limited to those involved in the hiring decision or who control access to the data. Also, with the exception of the drug and alcohol data, a motor carrier's insurer may have access to the data.

This data may only be used in the hiring decision.

The file must include a copy of your written authorization for the motor carrier to see information about your drug and alcohol history.

The file must also include a copy of responses received regarding the investigation by the previous employer or documentation of good faith efforts to contact the previous employer. The record must include the previous employer's name and address, the date the previous employer was contacted, and the information received about the driver from the previous employer.

Failure to contact the previous employer or failure of the previous employer to provide the required safety performance history information must be documented.

If you are hired, the safety performance histories received from previous employers must be kept for as long as you work for the employer and for an additional 3 years after you leave the employer.

The employer must make all of these records available to an agent or authorized FMCSA representative upon request.

Subpart G — Limited Exemptions

§391.61 Drivers who were regularly employed before January 1, 1971.

If you have worked for the same employer as a single-employer driver since January 1, 1971, or earlier, there are certain items your employer doesn't need to keep in your driver qualification file including:

√ application for employment (§391.21);

√ motor vehicle record from states (§391.23);

√ previous employer information (§391.23); and

√ road test form and certificate or equivalent (§391.31 and §391.33).

§391.63 Multiple-employer drivers.

A multiple-employer driver is defined as a driver, who in any period of 7 straight days, is employed or used as a driver by **more** than one motor carrier (*see §390.5*).

If a motor carrier hires you as a multiple-employer driver, the motor carrier must comply with all of the requirements in Part 391 with the following exceptions. The motor carrier is not required to:

√ make you furnish an employment application (§391.21);

√ make investigations/inquiries (§391.23);

√ perform the annual driving record inquiry (§391.25(a));

√ perform the annual review of your driving record (§391.25(b)); or

√ require you to furnish a record of violations or certificate (§391.27).

Before the motor carrier allows you to drive a commercial motor vehicle the carrier must obtain your name, Social Security number, and the type and issuing state of your commercial motor vehicle operator's license.

The motor carrier must keep the information listed above in its files for 3 years after your employment by the motor carrier ends.

§391.65 Drivers furnished by other motor carriers.

A motor carrier may use you, a driver who is regularly employed by another motor carrier, without following the driver qualification file requirements, if your regular employer certifies that you are fully qualified to drive a commercial motor vehicle. This certificate must include a statement which:

√ is signed and dated by your regular employer;

√ contains your name and signature;

√ certifies that you are regularly employed as defined in §390.5;

√ certifies that you are fully qualified to drive a commercial motor vehicle under the rules of Part 391 of the Federal Motor Carrier Safety Regulations;

√ states the expiration date of your medical exam certificate;

√ lists an expiration date for the certificate (either up to 2 years or the expiration date on the medical certificate); and

√ follows the format of the following form.

(Name of driver)   (SS No.)

(Signature of driver)

I certify that the above named driver, as defined in §390.5 is regularly driving a commercial motor vehicle operated by the below named carrier and is fully qualified under Part 391, Federal Motor Carrier Safety Regulations. His current medical examiner's certificate expires on _____
                                                  (Date)

This certificate expires: _____
       (Date not later than expiration date of medical certificate)

Issued on _____
                                    (Date)

Issued by _____
                      (Name of carrier)

(Address)

(Signature)   (Title)

The motor carrier that receives this certificate must contact your regular employer to verify that the certificate is true and accurate. This contact may be made by phone, by letter, or in person.

The employer that certifies your qualifications is responsible for the accuracy of your certificate.

The certificate is no longer valid if you leave your regular employer or if you are no longer qualified to drive a commercial motor vehicle under Part 391.

The motor carrier that gets the certificate must keep a copy in its files for 3 years.

§391.67 Farm vehicle drivers of articulated commercial motor vehicles.

Editor's Note: A farm vehicle driver is defined as a person who only drives a commercial motor vehicle that is:

√ controlled and operated by a farmer as a private carrier of property;

√ being used to transport either agricultural products or farm machinery, farm supplies, or both, to or from a farm;

√ not being used in the operation of a for-hire motor carrier;

√ not carrying hazardous materials in a type or amount that requires placarding; and

√ being used within 150 air-miles of the farmer's farm.

The following rules do not apply if you are a farm vehicle driver who is at least 18 years old and you drive an articulated commercial motor vehicle:

√ §391.11(b)(1), (b)(6), and (b)(8) (relating to driver qualifications);

√ Subpart C (relating to disclosure of, investigation into, and inquiries about your background, character, and driving record);

√ Subpart D (relating to road tests); and

√ Subpart F (relating to maintenance of files and records).

PART 392 — DRIVING OF COMMERCIAL MOTOR VEHICLES

The **_exact wording_** of the regulations in this section appears in Part 392 of the Federal Motor Carrier Safety Regulations.

Editor's Note: You must comply with all of the Part 392 regulations if you drive a vehicle that:

√ has a gross vehicle weight rating (GVWR), gross combination weight rating (GCWR), gross vehicle weight (GVW), or gross combination weight (GCW) of 10,001 pounds or more (whichever is greater);

√ is designed or used to transport more than 15 passengers (including the driver);

√ is designed or used to transport between 9 and 15 passengers (including the driver) for direct compensation, provided the vehicle is being operated beyond a 75 air-mile radius (86.3 statute miles) of your normal work reporting location; or

√ transports a placardable amount of hazardous materials.

Subpart A — General

§392.1 Scope of the rules in this part.

All employees of your company must be instructed in and follow the rules in Part 392.

§392.2 Applicable operating rules.

When driving a commercial motor vehicle, you must follow all of the rules of the area that you are traveling through. However, if a regulation of the Federal Motor Carrier Safety Administration (FMCSA) is stricter, the FMCSA regulation must be followed.

§392.3 Ill or fatigued operator.

You may not drive a commercial motor vehicle, and your employer may not require or permit you to drive, if you are tired or sick and your fatigue or illness will affect your ability to drive safely.

§392.4 Drugs and other substances.

You may not be on duty and possess, be under the influence of, or use, any illegal drugs or any substances that would make you unable to safely operate a commercial motor vehicle.

For the purposes of Part 392, "possession" does not include possession of a substance which is manifested and transported as part of a shipment.

Exception — The only time you may be allowed to possess or use a drug is if it is ordered by your doctor and won't affect your ability to drive safely.

§392.5 Alcohol prohibition.

As a driver, you may not:

√ use alcohol (as defined in §382.107) or be under the influence of alcohol within 4 hours before going on duty;

√ use or be under the influence of alcohol while on duty or driving a commercial motor vehicle;

√ be on duty or drive a commercial motor vehicle while possessing wine, beer, or distilled spirits. (This does not apply to possession of wine, beer, or distilled spirits which are manifested and transported as part of a shipment.)

Your employer may not require or permit you to be on duty or operate a commercial motor vehicle if you appear to have used alcohol within the past 4 hours.

If you are in violation of any of the provisions listed above you will be placed out of service immediately for a period of 24 hours. The 24-hour out-of-service period will begin once the out-of-service order is issued.

§392.6

If you are issued an out-of-service order, you must inform your employer of the out-of-service order within 24 hours and you must report it to the state which issued your driver's license within 30 days.

§392.6 Schedules to conform with speed limits.

You are required to follow the posted speed limits at all times. Your employer may not schedule a run that would require you to travel at speeds greater than the speed limit.

§392.7 Equipment, inspection, and use.

You must be sure that the following parts and accessories are in good working order before operating your commercial motor vehicle:

√ service brakes, including trailer brake connections;

√ parking (hand) brake;

√ steering mechanism;

√ lighting devices and reflectors;

√ tires;

√ horn;

√ windshield wiper or wipers;

√ rear-vision mirror or mirrors; and

√ coupling devices.

§392.8 Emergency equipment, inspection, and use.

You must be sure that all emergency equipment required in §393.95 is in place and in good working order before you start a trip. You are also required to use the emergency equipment when needed.

§392.9 Safe loading.

Make sure your cargo is loaded so it won't spill or shift. The cargo must not block your view of the road. The cargo may not block cab doors or emergency equipment.

The cargo should be checked:

√ within 50 miles of the start of your trip;

√ when you make a change of duty status, after your vehicle has been driven for 3 hours, or 150 miles, whichever comes first.

Exception — You are not to check sealed cargo if you have been ordered not to.

§392.9a Operating authority.

Vehicles providing transportation requiring operating authority must not be operated and will be placed out of service if the motor carrier operates the vehicles:

√ without the required operating authority; or

√ beyond the scope of the operating authority granted.

In addition, the motor carrier may be subject to penalties in accordance with 49 U.S.C. 14901.

Motor carriers placed out of service may have the out-of-service order reviewed within 10 days of its issuance.

Subpart B — Driving of Vehicles

§392.10 Railroad grade crossings; stopping required.

If you are driving one of the following vehicles:

1. A bus transporting passengers.

2. A commercial motor vehicle transporting any quantity of a Division 2.3 chlorine.

3. A commercial motor vehicle required to be marked or placarded with one of the following markings:

   √ Division 1.1;

   √ Division 1.2, or Division 1.3;

√ Division 2.3 Poison gas;

√ Division 4.3;

√ Class 7;

√ Class 3 Flammable;

√ Division 5.1;

√ Division 2.2;

√ Division 2.3 Chlorine;

√ Division 6.1 Poison;

√ Division 2.2 Oxygen;

√ Division 2.1;

√ Class 3 Combustible liquid;

√ Division 4.1;

√ Division 5.1;

√ Division 5.2;

√ Class 8; or

√ Division 1.4.

4. A cargo tank motor vehicle, whether loaded or empty, used for the transportation of any hazardous material as defined in the Hazardous Materials Regulations (Parts 107 through 180).

5. A cargo tank motor vehicle transporting a commodity which at the time of loading has a temperature above its flash point as determined by §173.120.

6. A cargo tank motor vehicle, whether loaded or empty, transporting any commodity under exemption in accordance with the provisions of Part 107 Subpart B.

You may not cross a railroad track or tracks at grade unless you first:

√ stop your commercial motor vehicle between 15 feet and 50 feet of the tracks;

√ listen and look in each direction along the tracks for an approaching train; and

√ make sure that no train is approaching.

When it is safe to do so, you may drive your commercial motor vehicle across the tracks. You may not shift gears while crossing the tracks.

There are also certain places where you are not required to stop, including:

√ a streetcar crossing, or railroad tracks used exclusively for industrial switching purposes, within a business district;

√   a railroad grade crossing when a police officer or crossing flagman directs traffic to proceed;

√   a railroad grade crossing, controlled by a traffic signal that is green;

√   an abandoned railroad grade crossing which is marked with a sign indicating that the rail line is abandoned; and

√   an industrial or spur line railroad grade crossing marked with a sign reading "Exempt."

§392.11 Railroad grade crossings; slowing down required.

If you are hauling cargo that is not listed in §392.10 and you reach a railroad crossing, you must slow your vehicle to a rate of speed that will allow you to stop before reaching the first rail.

§392.14 Hazardous conditions; extreme caution.

You are required to use extra caution when ice, snow, sleet, fog, mist, rain, dust, or smoke make it hard for you to see or control your vehicle. If conditions are hazardous you must stop and may not start again until you can safely operate your vehicle.

§392.16 Use of seat belts.

If your commercial motor vehicle has a seat belt assembly, you must use it at all times.

Subpart C — Stopped Vehicles

§392.22 Emergency signals; stopped commercial motor vehicles.

If your vehicle is stopped on the traveled portion or shoulder of a highway for any reason (other than a necessary traffic stop), you must immediately turn on your vehicle's two front and two rear signals as a hazard warning.

You must set out emergency warning devices within 10 minutes.

The placement of warning devices varies. The following table shows how warning devices should be placed depending on the type of road.

If road type is...	Then placement of devices is...
Two-lane road	On the traffic side of the vehicle 4 paces (approximately 10 feet or 3 meters) from the front or rear, depending on traffic direction. Also place a device 40 paces (approximately 100 feet or 30 meters) behind and a device 40 paces (approximately 100 feet or 30 meters) ahead of your vehicle on the shoulder or in the lane the vehicle is in.
Within 500 feet of a hill, curve or obstruction	100 to 500 feet from the vehicle in the direction of the obstruction. Place the other two according to the rules for two-lane or divided highways.
One-way or divided highway	10, 100, and 200 feet of the rear of the vehicle, toward the approaching traffic.

Do not place fusees where material that can burn or explode is leaking.

You are not required to set out warning devices if your vehicle is stopped within the business or residential district of a city when there is enough daylight or street lighting to give oncoming drivers a clear view of your truck.

§392.24 Emergency signals; flame producing.

You may not attach a lighted fusee or other flame-producing emergency signal to your commercial motor vehicle.

§392.25 Flame producing devices.

Use of flame-producing devices is prohibited if your vehicle:

√ carries Division 1.1, 1.2, 1.3 explosives;

√ is a cargo tank motor vehicle used for the transportation of Division 2.1 or Class 3 hazardous materials whether loaded or empty; or

√ is a commercial motor vehicle using compressed gas as a motor fuel.

Instead of using flame-producing devices, emergency reflective triangles, red electric lanterns, or red emergency reflectors must be used.

Subpart D — Use of Lighted Lamps and Reflectors

§392.33 Obsured lamps or reflectors.

You may not drive your vehicle it its lamps or reflectors are blocked by the tailboard, a part or the load, or dirt.

Subpart F — Fueling Precautions

§392.50 Ignition of fuel; prevention.

You or any other employee of your company may not:

√ fuel a commercial motor vehicle with the engine running;

√ smoke or expose an open flame while fueling a commercial motor vehicle;

√ fuel a commercial motor vehicle if the nozzle of the fuel hose is not in contact with the intake pipe of the fuel tank at all times; or

√ allow anyone else to do anything dangerous that could cause a fire or explosion.

Subpart G — Prohibited Practices

§392.60 Unauthorized persons not to be transported.

You may not transport anyone in your commercial motor vehicle unless your employer has given you written permission. The written permission must include the name of the person being transported, where your trip will begin and end, and the date when this permission expires.

Written permission is not necessary for:

√ employees or other people assigned to a commercial motor vehicle by your employer;

√ anyone being transported in the case of an accident or other emergency;

√ an attendant assigned to care for livestock.

Exception — This requirement does not apply to commercial motor vehicles operated and controlled by a farmer and used for the transportation of agricultural commodities or products to and from his/her farm or in the transportation of supplies to his/her farm.

§392.62 Safe operation, buses.

You may not drive a bus unless:

√ all standees are behind the standee line (*see §393.90*);

√ all aisle seats conform with §393.91; and

√ baggage and freight are stowed and secured so you can move freely, all exits are clear, and passengers can't be hit by items carried in the bus.

§392.63 Towing or pushing loaded buses.

A disabled bus with passengers aboard may not be towed or pushed. A bus with passengers aboard may not be used to tow or push a disabled motor vehicle.

Exception — The only exception to this provision is when the hazard to passengers would be greater if the towing or pushing of the vehicle did not occur. Then the bus may only be towed or pushed to the nearest point where the safety of passengers is assured.

§392.64 Riding within closed commercial vehicles without proper exits.

You or a passenger may not ride within the closed body of a commercial motor vehicle unless there is an exit. The exit door must be easy to open from inside.

§392.66 Carbon monoxide; use of commercial motor vehicle when detected.

A commercial motor vehicle may not be dispatched and you may not drive it when:

√ an occupant in the vehicle has been affected by carbon monoxide;

√ carbon monoxide has been detected inside the vehicle; or

√ a mechanical condition that could produce carbon monoxide has been discovered.

You may not drive the commercial motor vehicle until the problem has been repaired.

§392.67 Heater, flame-producing; on a commercial motor vehicle in motion.

An open flame heater used in the loading or unloading of goods may not be used when your vehicle is moving.

§392.71 Radar detectors; use and/or possession.

You may not use or have a radar detector in your commercial motor vehicle. Your employer may not require you to use a radar detector in your commercial motor vehicle.

PART 395 — HOURS OF SERVICE OF DRIVERS

The *exact wording* of the regulations in this section appears in Part 395 of the Federal Motor Carrier Safety Regulations.

Editor's Notes: You must comply with all of the Part 395 regulations if you drive a vehicle that:

√ has a gross vehicle weight rating (GVWR), gross combination weight rating (GCWR), gross vehicle weight (GVW), or gross combination weight (GCW) of 10,001 pounds or more (whichever is greater);

√ is designed or used to transport more than 15 passengers (including the driver);

√ is designed or used to transport between 9 and 15 passengers (including the driver) for direct compensation, provided the vehicle is being operated beyond a 75 air-mile radius (86.3 statute miles) of your normal work reporting location; or

√ transports a placardable amount of hazardous materials.

The term on-duty time is used throughout Part 395. On-duty time is defined as all time from the time you begin to work or are required to be ready to work until you are relieved from all work and responsibility for doing work. On-duty time includes:

√ all time at a plant, terminal, facility, or other property of a motor carrier or shipper, or on any public property, waiting to be dispatched, unless you have been relieved from duty by your motor carrier;

√ all time inspecting, servicing, or conditioning any commercial motor vehicle at any time;

√ all driving time (defined as all time spent at the controls of a commercial motor vehicle in operation);

√ all time, other than driving time, in or upon any commercial motor vehicle except time spent resting in a sleeper berth;

√ all time loading or unloading a commercial motor vehicle, supervising, or assisting in the loading or unloading, attending a commercial motor vehicle being loaded or unloaded, remaining in readiness to operate the commercial motor vehicle, or in giving or receiving receipts for shipments loaded or unloaded;

√ all time repairing, obtaining assistance, or remaining in attendance upon a disabled commercial motor vehicle;

√ all time spent providing a breath sample or urine specimen, including travel time to and from the collection site, in order to comply with drug and alcohol testing requirements in Part 382 when directed by a motor carrier;

√ performing any other work in the capacity, employ, or service of, a motor carrier; and

√ performing any compensated work for a person who is not a motor carrier.

§395.1 Scope of the rules in this part.

Part 395 applies to all motor carriers and drivers. Exceptions for specific situations are covered in §395.1.

Adverse driving conditions. If driving conditions are poor and you cannot safely complete a run within the 11 hours maximum driving time (property-carrying vehicle) or 10 hours maximum driving time (passenger-carrying vehicle) you may drive for up to 2 extra hours to complete the run or reach a safe place to stop.

Adverse driving conditions mean snow, sleet, fog, or unusual road and traffic conditions that your dispatcher didn't know about at the time of dispatch.

Under this exception the driver of a property-carrying vehicle may not drive:

√ for more than 13 hours following 10 consecutive hours off duty; or

√ at the end of the 14th consecutive hour since coming on duty following 10 consecutive hours off duty.

Under this exception the driver of a passenger-carrying vehicle may not drive:

√ for more than 12 hours following 8 consecutive hours off duty; or

√ after 15 hours of on-duty time following 8 consecutive hours off duty.

Driver-salesperson. If you are a driver-salesperson and you drive less than 40 hours in 7 consecutive days, your on-duty time isn't limited by the hours-of-service rules. (*See the*

*Federal Motor Carrier Safety Regulations to
be sure you qualify.)*

100 air-mile radius driver. As the driver of
a property-carrying vehicle, you are not required to make out a log if the following criteria are met:

√   you must drive within a 100 air-mile radius of your normal work reporting location;

√   you must return to your work reporting
location and be released from work within 12 consecutive hours;

√   you must have at least 10 consecutive
hours off duty separating each 12 hours
on duty;

√   you do not drive more than 11 hours following 10 consecutive hours off duty; and

√   your employer keeps your time records
for 6 months showing the time you report
for duty and are released from duty each
day, the total number of hours you are on
duty each day, and the total time you are
on duty for the past seven days if you are
used for the first time or intermittently.

§395.1

As the driver of a passenger-carrying vehicle, you are not required to make out a log if the following criteria are met:

√ you must drive within a 100 air-mile radius of your normal work reporting location;

√ you must return to your work reporting location and be released from work within 12 consecutive hours;

√ you must have at least 8 consecutive hours off duty separating each 12 hours on duty;

√ you do not drive more than 10 hours following 8 hours off duty; and

√ your employer keeps your time records for 6 months showing the time you report for duty and are released from duty each day, the total number of hours you are on duty each day, and the total time you are on duty for the past 7 days if you are used for the first time or intermittently.

Short-haul operations — As the driver of a property-carrying commercial motor vehicle, you may extend your workday twice in any period of 7 consecutive days and are not required to maintain a record of duty status (driver's log) if the following criteria are met:

√ you are not required to hold a commercial driver's license (CDL) to operate your vehicle; and

√ you remain within a 150 air-mile radius of your normal work reporting location and return to and are released from your normal work reporting location at the end of each day.

Under this exception you must not drive:

√ after the 14th hour after coming on duty on 5 days of any period of 7 consecutive days; and

√ after the 16th hour after coming on duty on 2 days of any period of 7 consecutive days.

When involved in short-haul operations you must:

√ comply with the 11-hour driving rule;

√ have at least 10 consecutive hours off duty separating each on-duty period; and

√ comply with the 60-hour/7-day limit or 70-hour/8-day limit (you may use the 34-hour restart provision if applicable).

You are not required to keep a record of duty status (driver's log), but your employer is required to keep a time record showing the time you report for and are released from duty each day, the total number of hours you are on duty each day and the total time you are on duty for the past 7 days if you are used for the first time or intermittently.

If you use this exemption you are not eligible to use the 100 air-mile radius exception, the sleeper-berth exception, or the property-carrying driver (16-hour) exemption.

Retail store deliveries. If you are making local deliveries from retail stores and/or retail catalog businesses to consumers during the Christmas rush (December 10 to December 25) and drive within a 100-air mile radius of your work reporting location, you do not have to follow the 11 hour driving time and 14 consecutive hour on-duty regulations.

Sleeper berths - property-carrying commercial motor vehicles — As the driver of a property–carrying commercial motor vehicle, you must, before driving, accumulate:

√ at least 10 consecutive hours off duty;

√ at least 10 consecutive hours of sleeper-berth time; or

√ a combination of consecutive sleeper-berth and off-duty time amounting to at least 10 hours.

You can also use the split sleeper-berth option to obtain the equivalent of 10 consecutive hours off duty, providing:

√ one sleeper-berth period is at least 8 (but less that 10) consecutive hours; and

√ a separate period of at least 2 (but less than 10) hours is spent in the sleeper berth, off duty, or any combination of the two.

Calculation of driving time includes all driving time. Compliance must be re-calculated from the end of the first of the two periods.

Calculation of the 14-hour limit includes all time except any sleeper-berth period of at least 8 but less than 10 consecutive hours. Compliance must be re-calculated from the end of the first of the two periods.

Sleeper berths - oil field operations — As the specially trained driver of a specially constructed oil well servicing commercial motor vehicle at a natural gas or oil well location, you may accumulate the equivalent of 10 consecutive hours of off-duty time by taking a combination of at least 10 consecutive hours of off-duty time, sleeper-berth time, or time in other sleeping accommodations at a natural gas or oil well location; or by taking two periods of rest in a sleeper berth or other sleeping accommodations at a natural gas or oil well location providing:

√ neither rest period is shorter than 2 hours;

√ the driving time in the period immediately before and after each rest period, when added together, does not exceed 11 hours; and

√ you do not drive after the 14th hour after coming on duty following 10 hours off duty, where the 14th hour is calculated:

1. By excluding any sleeper berth or other sleeping accomodation period of at least 2 hours which, when added to a subsequent (future) sleeper berth or other sleeping accommodation period totals at least 10 hours; and

2. By including all on-duty time, all off-duty time *not* spent in the sleeper berth or other sleeping accommodations, all such periods of less than 2 hours, and any period not described in number one (1.).

You may not return to driving under the nor mal limits listed in §395.3 without taking:

√ at least 10 consecutive hours off duty;

√ at least 10 consecutive hours in the sleeper berth or other sleeping accommodations; or

√ a combination of at least 10 consecutive hours of off-duty, sleeper-berth time, or time in other sleeping accommodations.

Sleeper berths - passenger carrying commercial motor vehicle — As the driver of a passenger-carrying commercial motor vehicle, you may accumulate the equivalent of 8 consecutive hours of off-duty time by taking a combination of at least 8 consecutive hours of off-duty *and* sleeper berth time; or by taking two periods of rest in the sleeper berth providing:

√ neither period is shorter than 2 hours;

√ the driving time in the period immediately before and after each rest period, when added together, does not exceed 10 hours; and

√ the on-duty time in the period immediately before and after each rest period, when added together, does not include any driving time after the 15th hour.

You may not return to driving under the normal limits listed in §395.5 without taking:

√ at least 8 consecutive hours off duty;

√ at least 8 consecutive hours in the sleeper berth; or

√ a combination of at least 8 consecutive hours of off-duty and sleeper-berth time.

State of Alaska. If you are driving a property-carrying commercial motor vehicle in Alaska you may not drive:

√ more than 15 hours following 10 consecutive hours off duty; or

√ after being on duty for 20 hours or more following 10 consecutive hours off duty.

You may not drive after having been on duty for:

√ 70 hours in any period of 7 consecutive days if your company does not operate every day of the week; or

√ 80 hours in any period of 8 consecutive days if your company operates every day of the week.

If you are driving a property-carrying commercial motor vehicle in Alaska and come upon adverse driving conditions, you may drive until the run is completed. After you complete the run, you must have at least 10 consecutive hours off duty before driving again.

If you are driving a passenger-carrying commercial motor vehicle in Alaska you may not drive:

√ more than 15 hours after 8 consecutive hours off duty;

√ after being on duty for 20 hours or more following 8 consecutive hours off duty;

√ after having been on duty for 70 hours in any period of 7 consecutive days, if your company does not operate vehicles every day of the week;

√ after having been on duty for 80 hours in any period of 8 consecutive days, if your company operates vehicles every day of the week.

If you are driving in Alaska and come upon adverse driving conditions you may drive until the run is completed. After you complete the run you must have 8 consecutive hours off duty before driving again.

State of Hawaii. If you drive in Hawaii, the record of duty status rules found in §395.8 do not apply if your employer keeps for 6 months, records showing:

√ the total number of hours you are on duty each day; and

√ the time you report for, and are released from, duty each day.

Travel time. When you, (a driver of a property-carrying commercial motor vehicle) at the direction of your employer are traveling, but are not driving or have any other responsibility to your employer, you must count this time as on-duty time. If you get at least 10 consecutive hours off duty once you have arrived at your destination, you may count all of the time, including the travel time, as off duty.

When you, the driver of a passenger-carrying commercial motor vehicle, at the direction of your employer are traveling, but are not driving or have any other responsibility to your employer, you must count this time as on-duty time. If you get at least 8 consecutive hours off duty once you have arrived at your destination you may count all of the time, including the traveling time, as off duty.

Agricultural operations. The hours-of-service regulations (all of Part 395) do not apply if you are transporting agricultural commodities or farm supplies for agricultural purposes within a state if the transportation is:

√ limited to a 100 air mile radius from the source of the commodities or distribution point for the farm supplies; and

√ conducted (except in the case of livestock feed transporters) during the planting and harvesting seasons as determined by the state.

The hours-of-service regulations (all of Part 395) do not apply at any time of year if you are a livestock feed hauler. (*See the Federal Motor Carrier Safety Regulations to be sure you qualify.*)

Ground water well drilling operations. If you drive a commercial motor vehicle that is used primarily in the transportation and operations of a ground water well drilling rig and are off duty for at least 24 consecutive

§395.1

hours, your period of 7 or 8 days ends at the beginning of your off-duty time. (*See the Federal Motor Carrier Safety Regulations to be sure you qualify.*)

Construction materials and equipment. If you drive a commercial motor vehicle that is used primarily in the transportation of construction materials and equipment, you may restart your 7 or 8 day clock after an off-duty period of at least 24 consecutive hours.

The transportation of construction materials and equipment is defined as the transportation of construction and pavement materials, construction equipment, and construction maintenance vehicles by a driver, to or from an active construction site within a 50 air-mile radius of the normal work reporting location of the driver. This exemption does not apply to drivers transporting placardable amounts of hazardous materials. (*See the Federal Motor Carrier Safety Regulations to be sure you qualify.*)

Utility service vehicles. The hours-of-service regulations (all of Part 395) do not apply if you drive a utility service vehicle. (*See the Federal Motor Carrier Safety Regulations to be sure you qualify.*)

Property-carrying driver (16-hour exemption). You (the driver of a property-carrying commercial motor vehicle) are allowed to accumulate 11 hours of driving time within 16 consecutive hours on duty once every 7 days provided you:

√   return to your normal work reporting location on that day, and are released from that work reporting location for the previous 5 on-duty days;

√   are released from duty within 16 hours of coming on duty (no additional on-duty time after 16 hours); and

√   have not taken this exemption within the previous 6 consecutive days (unless you have complied with the 34-hour voluntary "restart" provision).

Commercial motor vehicle transportation to or from a motion picture production site. If you drive a commercial motor vehicle that transports property or passengers to or from a theatrical or television motion picture production site within a 100 air-mile radius of your normal work reporting location you may not drive:

•   More than 10 hours following 8 consecutive hours off duty; or

- After having been on duty for 15 consecutive hours following 8 consecutive hours off duty.

If you drive beyond the 100 air-mile radius of your normal work reporting location, you may not use the provisions listed above.

Transporters of grapes during harvest period in the State of New York. The hours-of-service regulations (all of Part 395) do not apply if you transport grapes:

- within the state of New York;

- west of Interstate 81;

- within a 150 air-mile radius of where the grapes were picked or distributed; and

- during the state's harvest period.

§395.3 Maximum driving time for property-carrying vehicles.

After 10 consecutive hours off duty, you may not drive for more than 11 hours. You may not drive again until you have been off duty for another 10 consecutive hour period.

You may not drive after having been on duty for 14 consecutive hours. You may not drive again until you have at least 10 consecutive hours off duty.

If your company does not operate commercial motor vehicles every day of the week, you may not drive after having been on duty for 60 hours in any continuous 7-day period.

If your company operates commercial motor vehicles every day of the week, you may not drive after having been on duty for 70 hours in any continuous 8-day period.

You may "restart" this period of 7 or 8 consecutive days if you go off duty for a period of 34 or more consecutive hours.

§395.5 Maximum driving time for passenger-carrying vehicles.

After 8 consecutive hours off duty, you may drive for 10 hours. You may not drive again until you have been off duty for another 8-hour period.

You may not drive after having been on duty for 15 hours or more. You may not drive again until you have 8 consecutive hours off duty.

If your company does not operate commercial motor vehicles every day of the week, you may not drive after having been on duty for 60 hours in any continuous 7-day period.

If your company operates commercial motor vehicles every day of the week, you may not drive after having been on duty for 70 hours in any continuous 8-day period.

§395.8 Driver's record of duty status.

You must keep a written record of duty status (log book). The record must cover every day, including days off.

Your record must cover 24 hours, your duty status for the entire day.

Your duty status record must be recorded on the grid as follows:

√   "off duty" or "OFF";

√   "sleeper berth" or "SB";

√   "driving" or "D"; and

√   "on-duty not driving" or "ON".

Off duty. Except for time resting in a sleeper berth, you must draw a continuous line between the appropriate time markers to show periods of time when you are not on duty, not required to be in readiness to work, and not under any responsibility for performing work.

Sleeper berth. You must draw a continuous line between the appropriate time markers to show periods of time when you are off duty, resting in a sleeper berth.

Driving. You must draw a continuous line between the appropriate time markers to show periods of time when you are driving. In §395.2, driving time is defined as all time

spent at the driving controls of a commercial
motor vehicle in operation.

On-duty not driving. You must draw a continuous line between the appropriate time
markers to show the periods of time when
you are on duty, but not driving. (*See the first
page of this chapter for the definition of on-
duty time.*)

For each change of duty status, the name of
the city, town, or village, with state abbreviation must be recorded in the remarks section.

If the change of duty status occurs at a location other than a city, town, or village, you
must show one of the following:

√ the highway number and the nearest
milepost followed by the name of the
nearest city, town, or village and state abbreviation;

√ the highway number and the name of the
service plaza followed by the name of the
nearest city, town, or village and state abbreviation; or

√ the highway numbers of the two nearest
intersecting roadways followed by the
name of the nearest city, town, or village
and state abbreviation.

§395.8

Editor's Note: The following is an example of how a driver's duty status should be recorded for a trip from Richmond, Virginia to Newark, New Jersey.

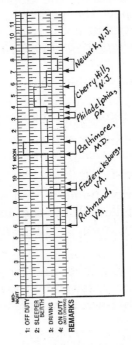

You must have an original and at least one copy of your record. All information must be true, current, and you must make all of your own entries (except for preprinted items).

You must include the following information in addition to the grid:

1. **Date.** You must write down the month, day, and year for the beginning of each 24-hour period.

2. **Total miles driving today.** You must record the total number of miles you drove during the 24-hour period.

3. **Truck or tractor and trailer number.** You must write down either the vehicle number(s) assigned by your company, or the license number and licensing state for each commercial motor vehicle operated during the 24-hour period.

4. **Name of carrier.** You must write down the name of the motor carrier you are working for. If you are working for more than one carrier in a 24-hour period you must list the times you started and finished work for each carrier.

5. **Driver's signature/certification.** You must certify that all of your entries are correct and true by signing your record of duty status, using your legal name or name of record.

6. **24-hour period starting time.** You must use the 24-hour period starting time designated by your home terminal. One hour increments must be preprinted, including "Noon" and "Midnight" spelled out.

7. **Main office address.** Your carrier's main office address must be on the record of duty status.

8. **Remarks.** This is the area where you must list the city, town, or village and state abbreviation when a change of duty status occurs.

9. **Name of co-driver.**

10. **Total hours.** You must list the total hours for each duty status (off duty, sleeper berth, driving, and on duty not driving) at the right of the grid. The total of the entries must equal 24 hours.

11. **Shipping document number(s), or name of shipper and commodity.**

Once you have completed a record of duty status, you have 13 days to forward the original copy to your employer.

Your employer must keep your records of duty status, and all supporting documents for at least 6 months.

You must keep a copy of each record of duty status in your possession for at least 7 consecutive days. The copies must be available for inspection by law enforcement at any time while you are on duty.

If you work for more than one motor carrier during a 24-hour period, you must submit a copy of your record of duty status to each motor carrier. The record must include:

√ all duty time for the entire 24-hour period;

√ the name of each motor carrier you worked for during the 24-hour period; and

√ the beginning and finishing time, including a.m. or p.m., worked for each motor carrier.

When a motor carrier uses you as a driver for the first time or intermittently, the motor carrier must get from you a signed statement showing your total time on duty during the past 7 days and the time you were last relieved from duty before beginning work for the motor carrier(s).

§395.13 Drivers declared out of service.

A law enforcement officer can ask for and look at your records at any time. If you have failed to keep your duty status record current on the day it is examined and the prior 7 days, you will be declared "out of service." You may not operate a commercial motor vehicle until you have had the appropriate number of consecutive hours off duty. This may include sleeper berth time.

If you are declared out of service you will be given a copy of the "Driver Out of Service Notice." You will receive a "Driver-Vehicle Examination Report" form. Mail this form to your employer within 24 hours. Your employer must return a portion of this form to the address on the form within 15 days.

§395.15 Automatic on-board recording devices.

Your employer may require you to use an automatic on-board recording device instead of a log book to keep track of your hours of service.

The on-board recording device must produce, on demand:

√   an hours-of-service chart;

√   electronic display; or

√ printout

showing the time and sequence of your duty status changes including your starting time at the beginning of each day.

The recording device must be able to produce your hours of service records upon demand when requested by a law enforcement official. This information may be used with handwritten or printed records of duty status for the past 7 days.

You must have in your possession, records of duty status for the past 7 consecutive days, available for inspection while on duty. The records must consist of information stored in and retrievable from the automatic on-board recording device, handwritten records, and/or computer generated records.

You must sign all hard copies of your record of duty status, certifying they are true and correct.

The following duty status information must be recorded by the on-board recording device:

√ "off-duty" or "OFF", or by an identifiable code or character;

√ "sleeper berth" or "SB", or by an identifiable code or character;

√ "driving" or "D", or by an identifiable code or character;

√ "on-duty not driving" or "ON", or by an identifiable code or character;

√ date;

√ total miles driving today;

√ truck or tractor and trailer number;

√ name of carrier;

√ main office address;

√ 24-hour period starting time;

√ name of co-driver;

√ total hours; and

√ shipping document number(s), or name of shipper and commodity.

For each change of duty status, you must record the name of the city, town, or village, and the state abbreviation. You may use location codes instead of listing the location name. If you use codes, a list of the codes must be kept in the cab of your vehicle and at your company's principal place of business. The list of codes must be made available to law enforcement officials on request.

If the automatic recording device isn't working properly, you must reconstruct (in writing) your record of duty status for the current day, and any of the past 7 days that you do not have records for. You must continue to prepare a handwritten record until the recording device is again working properly.

If you are using an on-board recording device you must keep in your vehicle an information packet including the following items:

√ an instruction sheet describing in detail how data may be stored and retrieved from the automatic on-board recording system; and

√ enough blank driver's records of duty status graph-grids for the entire time of your trip.

You must submit (either electronically or by mail) to your employer your records of duty status within 13 days following the completion of each record.

Make sure you review each record for accuracy before sending it to your employer. Your submission is certification that all entries are true and correct.

PART 396 — INSPECTION, REPAIR, AND MAINTENANCE

The ***exact wording*** of the regulations in this section appears in Part 396 of the Federal Motor Carrier Safety Regulations.

Editor's Note: You must comply with all of the Part 396 regulations if you drive a vehicle that:

√ has a gross vehicle weight rating (GVWR), gross combination weight rating (GCWR), gross vehicle weight (GVW), or gross combination weight (GCW) of 10,001 pounds or more (whichever is greater);

√ is designed or used to transport more than 15 passengers (including the driver);

√ is designed or used to transport between 9 and 15 passengers (including the driver) for direct compensation, provided the vehicle is being operated beyond a 75 air-mile radius (86.3 statute miles) of your normal work reporting location; or

√ transports a placardable amount of hazardous materials.

§396.1 Scope.

Your employer and all employees who directly deal with the inspection or maintenance of motor vehicles must understand and follow the regulations in Part 396.

§396.3 Inspection, repair, and maintenance.

Your employer must make sure all of your company's commercial motor vehicles are inspected and repaired. All parts and accessories must be in safe and proper operating condition at all times.

On buses, pushout windows, emergency doors, and emergency door marking lights must be inspected at least every 90 days.

If your employer has control of a vehicle for 30 days in a row or more, your company must keep the following information for each vehicle:

√   an identification of the vehicle including the company number (if your company assigns numbers to vehicles), make, serial number, year, and tire size (if the vehicle is not owned by your company, the name of the person furnishing the vehicle must be listed);

√ a way of showing the due date of various inspection and maintenance operations;

√ a record of inspection, repairs, and maintenance showing the date and nature of the inspection; and

√ for buses, a record of tests conducted on pushout windows, emergency doors, and emergency door marking lights.

The records mentioned in §396.3 must be kept where the vehicle is housed for at least 1 year. If your employer no longer owns or controls the vehicle the records must be kept for at least 6 months after the vehicle leaves your employer's control.

§396.5 Lubrication.

All commercial motor vehicles must be properly lubricated and free of oil and grease leaks.

§396.7 Unsafe operations forbidden.

You may not drive a vehicle if its condition is likely to cause an accident or breakdown.

§396.9 Inspection of motor vehicles in operation.

Authorized state and federal Department of Transportation (DOT) officials are allowed to perform vehicle inspections on the roadside and in some cases at company terminals. If an inspector finds that your vehicle's mechanical condition or the way it is loaded could cause an accident or breakdown, he/she can declare your vehicle out of service.

An "Out of Service Vehicle" sticker will be used to mark your vehicle out of service. No one may remove the out-of-service sticker until all of the repairs listed on the out-of-service notice are done.

If your vehicle is declared out of service, you may not drive it until all of the repairs listed on the out-of-service notice are done.

When you receive an inspection report at a roadside inspection the following must be done:

√ you must give this report to your employer as soon as you return to your terminal or facility (if you will not return to your terminal or facility in the next 24 hours, you must immediately mail the report to your employer);

√ your employer must repair any vehicle problems that were listed on the report; and

√ within 15 days your employer must complete, sign, and return the report to the agency that issued it, saying that any vehicle problems were corrected.

Your employer will keep a copy of this report at your company's principal place of business or where your vehicle is housed for at least 12 months after the date of the inspection.

§396.11 Driver vehicle inspection report(s).

You must complete and sign a written vehicle inspection report at the end of each day's work on each vehicle you drove. The report must cover at least the following parts and accessories:

√ service brakes including trailer brake connections;

√ parking (hand) brake;

√ steering mechanism;

√ lighting devices and reflectors;

√ tires;

√ horn;

√ windshield wipers;

√ rear vision mirror;

√   coupling devices;

√   wheels and rims; and

√   emergency equipment.

The report must identify the motor vehicle and list any defects or deficiencies that could cause an accident or breakdown. If you do not find any defects or deficiencies you must state this on the report. In all cases you must sign the report, showing you prepared the report. If you are working in a two-driver operation, only one driver needs to sign the report if you both agree on the vehicle's condition.

No specific format is required for the report, however provisions must be made for three signatures:

√   your signature, stating you prepared the report;

√   your motor carrier's or mechanic's signature certifying that the problems you reported have been corrected or that no correction is necessary; and

√   the reviewing driver's signature acknowledging the corrective action taken by the carrier.

§396.13

Your employer must keep the original of each driver vehicle inspection report and the certification of repairs for at least 3 months.

§396.13 Driver inspection.

Before driving a commercial motor vehicle you must:

√ be sure that the vehicle is in safe operating condition;

√ look over the last driver vehicle inspection report; and

√ if problems were listed on the report, review it and sign it if the problems were corrected.

§396.17 Periodic inspection.

Your commercial motor vehicle must pass an inspection at least once a year. The inspection must include the parts and accessories listed in Appendix G.

The inspection requirements may be met in many ways:

√ a state run inspection program;

√ a company run self-inspection program;

√ a roadside inspection; or

√ an inspection run by a commercial garage or similar business.

The inspection, performed by a qualified inspector, must meet federal or state standards.

The inspection must be documented by using an inspection report prepared according to the regulations in §396.21(a). A copy of the inspection report, or other forms of documentation based on the inspection report, including stickers or decals must be carried on the vehicle. If other forms of documentation are used they must include:

√ the date of the inspection;

√ name and address of the motor carrier or other place where the inspection report is kept;

√ information that identifies the vehicle inspected if it is not clearly marked on the vehicle; and

√ a certification that the vehicle has passed an inspection in accordance with §396.17.

If your vehicle's parts or accessories do not meet the minimum standards in Appendix G, your employer must repair them promptly.

§396.19 Inspector qualifications.

The person doing the annual inspection must:

√ understand the regulations;

√ know and be able to use the tools and equipment necessary to do an annual inspection; and

√ be trained or have a certain amount of experience doing annual inspections *(see §396.19.)*.

§396.21 Periodic inspection recordkeeping requirements.

The inspector must prepare an inspection report that includes:

√ the name of the person doing the inspection;

√ the carrier operating the vehicle;

√ the date of the inspection;

√ the vehicle inspected;

√ the parts of the vehicle inspected; and

√ certification that the report is accurate, complete, and follows the Part 396 requirements.

The original or a copy of the inspection report must be kept by the motor carrier or entity responsible for the inspection for at least 14 months. The inspection report must be kept where the vehicle is housed or maintained.

A copy of the inspection report, or a decal containing minimal information, must be on your vehicle.

§396.23 Equivalent to periodic inspection.

A commercial motor vehicle may meet the annual inspection requirements if it has been put through a roadside inspection in the past 12 months. If it has been put through a roadside inspection, your company must keep a copy of the inspection report showing the inspection was done according to the regulations.

A mandatory state inspection program may also be considered the same as an annual inspection.

§396.25 Qualifications of brake inspectors.

A brake inspector is defined as any person responsible for making sure that inspections, maintenance, repairs, or service to your vehicle's brakes meet federal safety standards. Your company is responsible for assigning only qualified people to inspect, maintain, repair, and service brakes.

The brake inspector must:

√ understand and be able to perform the brake service or inspection task;

√ know and be able to use the tools and equipment necessary to do a brake inspection; and

√ be trained or have a certain amount of experience doing brake inspections (*see* *§396.25*).

Your company must keep evidence of its brake inspector's qualifications at its principal place of business or where the brake inspector is employed. This paperwork must be kept for as long as the inspector is employed as a brake inspector plus an additional year.

PART 397 —
TRANSPORTATION OF
HAZARDOUS MATERIALS;
DRIVING AND PARKING
RULES

The **exact wording** of the regulations in this section appears in Part 397 of the Federal Motor Carrier Safety Regulations.

Subpart A — General

§397.1 Application of the rules in this part.

The rules in Part 397 must be followed if your employer transports hazardous materials that must be marked or placarded (*see §177.823*). The following people must follow the rules in Part 397:

√ your company's supervisors who deal with hazardous materials; and

√ any driver who deals with vehicles carrying hazardous materials.

§397.2 Compliance with federal motor carrier safety regulations.

When transporting hazardous materials that must be marked or placarded (*see §177.823*) you and your company must follow the regulations found in Parts 390 to 397.

§397.5 Attendance and surveillance of motor vehicles.

If you are hauling explosives (Division 1.1, 1.2, or 1.3), you cannot leave your truck unattended unless you meet all three of the following conditions:

1. You park your truck at one of these locations:

√   on your company's property;

√   on a shipper's or receiver's property;

√   in a safe haven; or

√   on a construction or survey site, if the truck is loaded with 50 pounds or less of explosives.

2. You make sure the person receiving the cargo knows what it is and what to do in an emergency.

3. You park the truck where you or the person receiving the cargo has a clear view of it.

If you are carrying hazardous materials that are not explosives, you cannot leave your truck unattended on a public street or highway or on the shoulder of a public highway. However, you may leave your truck unattended while performing duties that are necessary to operate your vehicle.

The following terms are used throughout Part 397:

1. **Attended** — A vehicle is attended when the person in charge of it is on the truck (awake and not in the sleeper berth) or has a clear view of the truck from no further than 100 feet.

2. **Qualified Representative** — A person who has been assigned to attend the truck. This person knows what is on the truck. He/she knows what to do in an emergency and can move the truck if necessary.

3. **Safe Haven** — An area where trucks hauling explosives can be parked unattended. These areas must be approved in writing by local, state, or U.S. government officials.

§397.7 Parking.

If you are hauling explosives (Division 1.1, 1.2, or 1.3) you may not park where there is possible danger to people or property. Do not park:

√ on the roadway;

√ within five feet of the roadway;

√ on private property (including restaurants and gas stations) without telling the person in charge about the cargo in your truck and getting permission from the person in charge;

√ within 300 feet of a bridge, tunnel, house, or any place where people work or get together (unless you absolutely must park there).

If you are hauling any other kind of hazardous material (other than Division 1.1, 1.2, or 1.3 materials) and you need to stop, you must park at least five feet from the highway, if at all possible.

§397.11 Fires.

If you are hauling hazardous materials you may not drive near an open fire unless you have taken precautions to make sure you can pass safely without stopping. If you are hauling hazardous materials you may not park within 300 feet of an open fire.

§397.13 Smoking.

You may not smoke or let anyone else smoke within 25 feet of a motor vehicle which contains Class 1 materials, Class 5 materials, or flammable materials classified as Division 2.1, Class 3, Divisions 4.1 and 4.2 or an empty tanker that was marked or placarded (*see §177.823*) because it hauled Class 3, flammable materials, or Division 2.1 flammable gases.

§397.15 Fueling.

The engine of your truck must be turned off when fueling. Someone must be in control of the fueling process.

§397.17 Tires.

You must check the tires:

√ before each trip, and

√ each time the truck is parked.

If a tire is flat, leaking, or improperly inflated do not continue your trip. Drive to the nearest safe place and get the tire fixed.

If a tire is overheated, remove it right away. Move the tire away from your truck, find out why it is overheating, and correct the problem before you drive again.

§397.19 Instructions and documents.

If you haul explosives (Division 1.1, 1.2, and 1.3), you must have a copy of the Part 397 rules and a document telling you what to do in the case of an accident or delay. The document must include:

√   the names and telephone numbers of the people (including the carrier and shipper) you should contact;

√   the type of explosives being transported; and

√   what emergency steps should be taken in the event of a fire, accident, or leak.

When you receive these documents you must sign a receipt. Your employer must keep the receipt for 1 year from the date you sign the receipt.

If you are hauling Division 1.1, 1.2, or 1.3 materials, you must have possession of and understand the documents listed above, the documents required in §177.817 and a written route plan (*see §397.67*).

Subpart C — Routing of Non-Radioactive Hazardous Materials

§397.67 Motor carrier responsibility for routing.

When hauling marked or placarded hazardous material (that is not a non-radioactive hazardous material (NRHM)), choose your route carefully.

You must avoid routes that go through or near:

√ heavily populated areas;

√ any place where crowds gather;

√ tunnels; and

√ narrow streets or alleys.

If you haul explosives (Divisoin 1.1, 1.2, and 1.3), you must have a written route plan before leaving. Your company or an agent of your company must write up the plan and give you a copy. If your trrip doesn't begin at the terminal, you can write up the plan.

SUBJECT INDEX

This index refers to the subjects included in the *Driver's Guide to the FMCSRs*. A complete subject index is located in the *Federal Motor Carrier Safety Regulations Pocketbook*.

A

Age of driver 391.11
Alcohol use and testing 382
Alcoholic beverages:
  Driving under the influence 383.51, 391.15, 392.5
  Driver's use of forbidden 392.5
  Excessive use of by drivers 391.15
  Penalties for use 383.51, 391.15

B

Brakes:
  Air brake knowledge requirements 383.121
  Inspector qualification 396.25
Bus:
  Commercial driver's license, passenger
    endorsement 383.117
  Loading 392.62
  Push out window inspection 396.3
  Towing or pushing when loaded prohibited .. 392.63

C

Carbon monoxide, vehicle use prohibited when
  present 392.66
Commercial driver's license 383.23
Commercial driver's license program 383
Commercial motor vehicle groups 383.91
Controlled substance testing: 382
  Post-accident testing requirements 382.303
  Pre-employment testing requirements 382.301
  Random testing 382.305
  Reasonable suspicion testing 382.307

D

Disabled vehicles, emergency signals for 392.22
Doctor's examination. (See Physical examination.)
Doubles/Triples endorsement 383.115
Driver:
  Alcoholic beverages, addiction 391.41
  Driving conditions, adverse 395.1
  Driving "out of service" vehicles 396.9
  Driving rules, compliance with State
    and local 392.2
  Driving unsafe vehicle prohibited 392.7
  Driving vehicle containing carbon monoxide . 392.66
  Driving while ill or fatigued 392.3
  Fueling precautions 392.50
  Hazardous conditions, caution 392.14
  Hours of service 395
  Inspection of emergency equipment 392.8
  Inspection of motor vehicle before driving ... 392.7
  Liquor, intoxicating 392.5
  Non-alcoholic drugs, addiction 391.41
  "Out of service," drivers 392.5, 395.13
  Prohibited nonalcoholic drugs.............. 392.4
  Record of duty status 395.8
  Vehicle inspection report 396.11
Driver license: 383
  Single license 383.21
  Notification requirements
    Violations, driver 383.31
    Suspensions 383.33
    Previous employment 383.35
    Employer responsibility 383.37
Federal disqualifications and penalties:
  Disqualification of drivers 383.51
Driver qualifications:
  Annual review of driving record 391.25
  Certificate of physical examination 391.43
  Driver, disqualification of 383.51, 391.15
  Driver qualification files 391.51
  Drivers, articulated (combination) farm
    vehicle 391.67
  Drivers, multiple-employer 391.63
  Drivers furnished by other motor carriers ... 391.65

Drivers, regularly employed prior to
   Jan. 1, 1971 .... 391.61
Duties of carrier-drivers 391.1
Employment, application for 383.35, 391.21
Exemptions, general 391.2
Investigation and inquiries 391.23
Medical examination; certificate of physical
   examination 391.43
Medical evaluations, conflict of 391.47
Persons who must be medically examined
   and certified 391.45
Physical qualifications 391.41
Qualifications of drivers 391.11
Qualifications, additional qualifications by
   carrier-driver permitted 391.1
Road test and certification 391.31
Road test, equivalent of 391.33
Violations, record of 391.27
Driver testing requirements: 383.71, 383.11
   Commercial driver's license document 383.151
   Required knowledge and skills 383.110,
      383.113
   Testing and licensing procedures 383.71, 383.73
   Tests 383.131
   Vehicle groups and endorsements 383.91, 383.93,
      383.115 thru
      383.119
Driving rules, compliance with State and local . 392.2
Driving rules, scope 392.1
Driving while ill or fatigued 392.3
Drug testing (see controlled substance testing)

E

Emergency signals:
   Flame-producing types, attachment to
      vehicles prohibited 392.24
   Flame-producing types, restrictions on use .. 392.25
   Placement of:
      Stopped vehicles 392.22
Employment application 383.35, 391.21
Exits from closed vehicles 392.64

F

Farm vehicle drivers 391.67
Fueling of vehicles, precaution 392.50

G

Grade crossings, precautions:
  Vehicles required to slow down 392.11
  Vehicles required to stop 392.10

H

Hazardous materials:
  Applicability of rules 397.1
  Attendance and surveillance of
    motor vehicles 397.5
  Compliance with Motor Carrier Safety
    Regulation 397.2
  Endorsement 383.121
  Fires 397.11
  Fueling 397.15
  Instructions and documents 397.19
  Parking 397.7
  Routes 397.9
  Smoking 397.13
  State and local laws, ordinances,
    and regulations 397.3
  Tires 397.17
Hitchhikers prohibited 392.60
Hours of service:
  Adverse driving conditions 395.1
  Automatic on-board recording devices 395.15
  Compliance required 395.1
  Drivers, declared "out of service" 395.13
  Drivers, record of duty status 395.8
  Emergency condition 395.1
  Maximum driving and on-duty time 395.3
  Sleeper berth 395.1
  Travel time 395.1

I

Inspection and maintenance:
  By driver-pretrip 392.7
  Compliance 396.1

Driver inspection 396.13
Equivalent to periodic inspection 396.23
Inspection, repair, and maintenance records . . . 396.3
Inspector qualifications: 396.19
    Operation of "out of service" vehicle
      prohibited 396.9
    Operation of unsafe vehicle prohibited 396.7
    "Out of service" vehicle forms 396.9
    Recordkeeping requirements 396.21
    Types of vehicle inspections (Periodic) 396.17
    Vehicle inspection report by driver 396.11
    Vehicles in operation 396.9
    Intoxicating beverages 392.5
Investigation and inquiries 391.23

L

License, revocation of 392.42
Lighting devices, dirty or obscured
    not permitted 392.33
Loading requirements, buses and trucks:
    Distribution and securing 392.9
    Fastenings, secure 392.9
    Not to interfere with driver 392.9
Logs (see Driver's record of duty status) 395.8

M

Maintenance (See Inspection and maintenance.)
Mental condition of driver 391.41
Motor vehicle, driving 392

N

Narcotics and dangerous substances 392.4

O

Operating authority ("out of service") 392.9a
Operating rules, applicability 392.2
"Out of service" drivers 395.13
"Out of service" vehicle forms 396.9
"Out of service" vehicles, operation prohibited . 396.9

P

Passenger endorsement 383.117
Passengers, unauthorized, prohibited 392.60

Physical condition of driver 391.41
Physical examination:
    Certificate 391.43
    Copy in carrier's file 391.51
    Copy in driver's possession 391.41
    Form 391.43
    Instructions for performing 391.43
    Periodic 391.45
    Persons who require 391.45
Physical requirements for drivers 391.41
Pretrip inspection 392.7

R

Radar detectors, prohibited 392.71
Railroad crossings:
    Slowing down for 392.11
    Stopping at 392.10
Road test: 391.31
    Certification of 391.31
    Equivalent of 391.33

S

Safe loading 392.9
Schedules to conform with speed limit 392.6
Seat belts, use 392.16
State regulations to be obeyed 392.2
Stopped vehicles:
    Emergency signals 392.22
    Precautions when left unattended 392.20

T

Tank vehicle endorsement 383.119
Turn signals:
    Disabled vehicles 392.22

U

Unsafe vehicle, operation prohibited 396.7

V

Violations, driving, record of 391.27

NOTES

NOTES

NOTES

NOTES

NOTES

NOTES

ORDER FORM

To order additional copies of this handbook, use the form below.

English Version Pricing		Spanish Version Pricing	
100-149 handbooks	$2.25 ea.	100-149 handbooks	$3.70 ea.
50-99 handbooks	$2.60 ea.	50-99 handbooks	$3.85 ea.
25-49 handbooks	$3.20 ea.	25-49 handbooks	$4.05 ea.
<25 handbooks	$3.40 ea.	<25 handbooks	$4.10 ea.

Contact Customer Service for pricing on additional quantities

PRICES SUBJECT TO CHANGE WITHOUT NOTICE

YES! Please send me:

☐ _____ copies of the *English Version* **Driver's Guide to the FMCSRs 2nd Edition** (HB 16 ORS) for only $ _____ ea.

☐ _____ copies of the *Spanish Version* **La guía del chofer para las FMCSRs segunda edición** (HB 16 ORS S) for only $ _____ ea.

That's a total of $ _____ .

Name _____ Title _____

Company _____

Street Address _____

P.O. Box _____

City _____ State _____ ZIP _____

Phone ( ) _____ Ext. _____

Fax ( ) _____

Purchase Order Number (if applicable) _____

☐ **Payment Enclosed.** (Include $7.95 shipping & handling. Add all applicable state and local sales tax except if shipping to AK, DC, DE, HI, MT, NH, NM, OR or WY.)

☐ **Please bill my company. (Minimum $50.00 order.** Subject to credit approval. $7.95 shipping & handling charges plus the actual freight charge will be added to your invoice. We reserve the right to add sales tax where required.)

☐ **Charge my:** ☐ 🅥🅘🅢🅐 ☐ ⬭ ☐ 🅐🅜🅔🅧 ($7.95 shipping & handling will be added. We reserve the right to add sales tax where required.)

Charge Card Acct. No. _____ Expiration Date _____

Authorized Signature _____

To order: copy, complete and mail this form.

J. J. Keller
& Associates, Inc.
3003 W. Breezewood Lane
P.O. Box 368
Neenah, WI 54957-0368
Since 1953

For immediate service, call toll-free

1-800-327-6868

Be sure to mention Action Code HB 96396

24-Hour Fax 1-800-727-7516
Order online at www.jjkeller.com